Tracking Significant Achievement in

PRIMARY SCIENCE

TRACKING
Significant
Achievement

in

Series editors: Shirley Clarke and Barry Silsby

PRIMARY SCIENCE

Esmé Glauert

Hodder & Stoughton
A MEMBER OF THE HODDER HEADLINE GROUP

Also published in this series:
Tracking Significant Achievement in Primary English
Tracking Significant Achievement in Primary Mathematics
Tracking Significant Achievement in the Early Years

Acknowledgements

Many thanks to the schools, teachers and their pupils who contributed samples for this book. I am particularly grateful to all the teachers who attended my course on significant achievement in Mathematics and Science in the Spring term of 1995.

British Library Cataloguing in Publication Data
A catalogue record for this title is available from the British Library

ISBN 0 340 65481 3
First published 1996

Impression number	10	9	8	7	6	5	4	3	2	1
Year		1999		1998		1997		1996		

Filmset by Wearset, Boldon, Tyne and Wear.
Printed in Great Britain for Hodder & Stoughton Educational, the educational publishing division of Hodder Headline Plc, 338 Euston Road, London NW1 3BH, by Bath Press, Bath, Avon.

Contents

1   Tracking Significant Achievement   7

2   Supporting Significant Achievement in Science   24

3   Significant Achievement in the Classroom   44

4   Development and Progression in Science   87

5   Some Common Questions Answered   101

6   Getting Started   113

1 Tracking Significant Achievement

by Shirley Clarke

The purpose of this book

With the advent of the revised National Curriculum, the focus for teachers' ongoing assessment has been to look for **significant achievement**, as opposed to looking for *all* aspects of achievement, which had been the previous practice.

This book, one of a series of four on significant achievement, aims to establish a coherent and manageable framework for organising ongoing assessment in the classroom, in which significant achievement is the focus. The underpinning principles for this are:

- ◆ the assessment process must include the child, aiming for the child to become part of the evaluation process;
- ◆ the assessment process must enhance the child's learning and the teachers' teaching;
- ◆ all assessment processes should be manageable.

This chapter describes good assessment practice, from the planning stage to assessment and record-keeping. It deals with the issue of defining significant achievement and how to look for it and recognise it.

Chapter 2 looks at good assessment practice within the context of science, so it considers good practice in science teaching, organisation and resource provision which will enable significant achievement to take place and to be recognised.

Chapter 3 provides a variety of examples of significant achievement, derived from teachers' work in the classroom, covering the range of age groups and the different aspects of significant achievement across Key Stage 1 and 2. It is hoped that, by the time you have read all these examples, you will have a very clear idea of what significant achievement in science might look like.

Chapter 4 sets out typical stages of significant achievement in science. The purpose of this is to provide basic guidance for teachers about which aspects of science are most important and significant in a child's development.

Chapter 5 has a question-and-answer format, covering all the issues that arose in a series of courses and during trialling carried out with teachers. It is followed by a final chapter on 'Getting Started'.

Defining assessment and its purpose

Mary Jane Drummond (1993) has a definition of assessment which clearly describes the process as it takes place in the classroom. She sets it out as three crucial questions which educators must ask themselves when they consider children's learning. Those questions are:

◆ *What is there to see?*
◆ *How best can we understand what we see?*
◆ *How can we put our understanding to good use?*

'What is there to see?' refers to the fact that we need to be able to access children's understanding in the best possible way. We need to be constantly talking to children about their work and maximising the opportunities for them to achieve in the first place and demonstrate their achievement in the second.

'How best can we understand what we see?' is the next stage. We need to be able to create a climate in the classroom where teachers are not simply hypothesising about the reasons for children's understanding, but have as much information as possible about a child's understanding,

coming from the child itself. We also need to be clear about the learning intentions of every activity, so that we know what we are looking for. We need to be flexible, however, because a child's achievement is not always directly related to the aims of the actual lesson. We need to remember that children learn from all their experiences of life, of which school learning is only a part.

'How can we put our understanding to good use?' is the key factor in moving children forwards. If the teacher has answered the first two questions, then the information gathered should give clear indications as to what should be the next move in helping a child to continue to progress.

The purpose of the assessment process is to make explicit children's achievements, celebrate their achievements with them, then help them to move forward to the next goal. Without children's involvement in the assessment process, assessment becomes a judgmental activity, resulting in a one-way view of a child's achievement. Information gathered in this way has minimal use. When shared with the child, assessment information is more likely to result in a raising of standards, because the child is more focused, motivated and aware of his or her own capabilities and potential. Good assessment practice enables children to be able to fulfil their learning potential and raises self-esteem and self-confidence.

'Assessment' can sometimes be used as the term for what is, in fact, record-keeping. It needs to be made clear that the assessment process is that outlined so far; a means of understanding children's understanding. Record-keeping is a follow-up to the assessment process, and needs to take place only when significant achievement has taken place. This will be described in some detail later. Evidence-gathering is part of the follow-up to assessment, and should be centred round the idea of a 'Record of Achievement' rather than a 'collection of evidence'. It is neither a statutory requirement (see both DFE/DFEE and SCAA documentation) nor useful to keep samples of children's work at set points in time as proof of National Curriculum attainment, whereas Records of Achievement are a motivating and useful aspect of the assessment process.

The planning, assessment and record-keeping cycle: a practical solution

The pre-planning stage

If assessment is to be worthwhile, it is clear that we must first maximise the opportunities for children's achievement, by giving them the best possible learning experiences. This can be achieved by a number of support structures in a school and by planning well in advance of the teaching.

Most primary schools have a 'curriculum framework' showing specific coverage of the Programmes of Study for 'blocked' work (e.g. history, geography, science and sometimes maths topics). These charts show who will cover what and in what term. I believe that knowing what it is you have to cover in this way aids planning and enables a school to set up resources of high quality in order to help teachers at the planning stage. Well managed, good quality topic boxes are an excellent idea, with the following as the ideal contents:

◆ artefacts, maps, charts, videos, reference books, tapes;
◆ teachers' previous plans;
◆ lists of local places to visit (e.g. nearby streets with good examples of Victorian houses) and museums, etc;
◆ lists of local facilities (e.g. loan packs from local libraries, etc);
◆ lists of people who can be used as a resource (e.g. artists in residence, local poets and historians, people who work in the school who have related interests and expertise);
◆ brainstorms of starting-point ideas for contextualising the topic (e.g. 'Colour' can be contextualised by creating an optician's shop in the classroom and covering what is needed through this).

With such resource support, teachers are more likely to create interesting, well-resourced topic plans, resulting in contexts in the classroom which enable children to learn more easily.

For ongoing aspects of the curriculum, such as language and maths, planning is focused much more around the scheme of work.

The planning stage

The single most important feature of good planning is to have well thought out learning intentions before any creation of activities. It is traditional practice in primary schools to have only the simplest notion of aims, then to launch into a brainstorm, resulting in a topic web of activities. Very often, it is the creation of so many activities which causes manageability problems for teachers. It can also lead to a ticklist approach, where getting through the activities is more important than responding to the way children react to them. It is children's learning which must be our main concern, *not* our plans or schemes of work. They should support the learning, not hinder it.

I suggest a method of planning which starts with more learning intentions and leads to only a few activities, all of which can be developed in depth, resulting in less superficial learning and a less frantic approach to coverage:

1   Find out what the children already know about the area to be covered, by brainstorm, open-ended problem or concept mapping. Brainstorming can be done with any age group. Simply say *'Next term we will be finding out about forces. What do you already know about forces?'* The resulting brainstorm will provide vital planning information for the teacher: the differentiation range – from the child who has only the simplest notion of what the word means, to the child who knows more about forces than the teacher! Having this means that activities can be planned which will meet the needs of all the abilities in the class if the two extremes have been defined.

2   Read the Programme of Study (PoS) statements.

3   Divide the topic, if necessary, into sub-headings – maybe two or three.

4   Create learning intentions, as follows, for each sub-heading:
   ◆ knowledge (*What do I want the children to know?*)
   ◆ skills (*What do I want the children to be able to do?*)
   ◆ concepts (*What do I want the children to understand?*)
   ◆ attitude (*What do I want the children to be aware of?*)
   ◆ equal opportunities (*What do I want the children to be aware of?*)

Clearly, the last two learning intentions lend themselves much more to geography, history or science topics than to maths topics, say, so should be used where appropriate.

An example of the process using FOOD as the topic to be covered, the context chosen to cover a science-based topic

Some appropriate sub-headings (after looking at the programmes of study) are *Nutrition* and *Cultural Differences*. For *Nutrition*, following the five aspects above, possible learning intentions might be:

◆ know the food groups (*knowledge*);
◆ be able to plan a healthy menu for a week (*skill*);
◆ understand the effect of diet on health (*concept*);
◆ be aware of the fact that we are able to control our health (*attitude*);
◆ be aware of the link between wealth and healthy eating (*equal opportunities*).

The same is then done for *Cultural Differences*. Learning intentions for Experimental and Investigative Science will usually feature more specifically, for particular children, in weekly plans, because of the ongoing nature of the programmes of study for this aspect of science. However, many schools take focused themes from the ongoing areas of the curriculum, such as *questioning* or *observation*, which means there will be a strong focus on that aspect while the rest of the ongoing area is covered at the same time. This would mean that there may be one or two further learning intentions in the list above, specifically focusing on Experimental and Investigative Science.

The next stage is to plan the activities the children will do. With such carefully defined learning intentions, teachers using this approach have said it makes the choice of activity much more focused than before. This in turn means that the teacher is absolutely clear about the purpose of the tasks children will do – a crucial step towards being able to create an evaluative ethos in the classroom. If the teacher is not clear why children are doing a task, the activity is likely to produce superficial results and a feeling of anxiety on the part of the teacher, who may feel that she does not know exactly what she is supposed to be expecting or looking for.

Making assessments in the classroom: setting up the assessment dialogue

Once the teacher is sure of the purpose of every task, the next step is to let children into the secret! By this, I mean, in words which they will understand, say why you want them to do the activity (e.g. *'This will help you learn more about which things dissolve best . . . I also want to see how well you can work with another person'*). This can be said to the whole class, a group, pairs or individuals, depending on how you set children off. The important thing about this is that it takes no more time than it does for the task itself to be explained; it simply needs to become a habit on the part of the teacher.

It is important that children are let into the secret, for two reasons:

◆ First, because knowing the purpose focuses the child towards a particular outcome. Very often, children have no idea why they have been asked to do something, and they can only look for clues or 'guess what's in the teacher's mind' as a means of knowing what is expected of them.
◆ Second, because they are being invited to take more control over evaluating their achievements. If the purpose is known, this is more likely to encourage the child to be weighing up the relative strengths and weaknesses of their work as they are doing it.

With children informed of the purpose of the task, the assessment agenda has been set, because, when children finish their work, or are spoken to in the middle of the task, the teacher can say *'How do you think you have got on with finding out about dissolving? What makes them dissolve quicker?'*. This does not mean that there should be a systematic attempt to speak to every child, as that would be unmanageable. Apart from setting children off and concluding a session, most of a teacher's time is spent talking to individual children, by going to see how they are getting on or by their coming to the teacher. So the time *does* exist when children can be asked about their progress. It does not need to be structured, set-aside time, but can become part of the ongoing dialogue teachers have with children all through the day. The 'assessment dialogue' is simply a *different* way of talking to the children. The advantage for the teacher in asking the children how they are doing in relation to the 'shared secret' or learning criteria is that it is a powerful strategy for accessing information about children's progress.

This type of questioning invites the child to play an active part in his/her learning. Children who are used to being asked such questions readily respond, giving honest answers, because they know the purpose of the teacher's questions is to help their learning process. The answers children give often put a teacher fully in the picture about the child's level of understanding as well as why something now appears to be understood (e.g. *'I understand this now'*, *'Lisa helped me with these two'*, *'I didn't want to work with Sam because I wanted to do it like this'*, etc).

This is the assessment process at its best. It describes the means by which the teacher makes all her ongoing decisions about children's learning and what they need to do next. Most of the insights gleaned from this continuous dialogue simply inform day-to-day decisions and it is unnecessary to record them. However, when significant achievement occurs, there is a need to recognise and record the event.

Making assessments in the classroom: looking for significant achievement and recording it

Record-keeping must have a purpose. If a teacher is to spend time writing things down, it must be useful to both teacher and child. If record-keeping is focused on children's significant achievement, it fulfils many purposes. First, however, we need to look closely at what significant achievement is.

Significant achievement is any leap in progress. It may be the first time a child does something (e.g. sitting still for more than five minutes), or it may be when the teacher is sure that a particular skill or concept has now been thoroughly demonstrated (e.g. in a number of contexts, shows an understanding that sounds are made when objects vibrate). Work with teachers has led us to believe that significant achievement falls into five categories:

◆ **physical skill** (e.g. use of tools);
◆ **social skill** (e.g. able to take turns);
◆ **attitude development** (e.g. increased confidence in problem-solving);
◆ **concept clicking/conceptual development** (e.g. clear understanding that some change is irreversible);
◆ **process skill** (e.g. able to offer explanations).

These are all examples of possible significant achievement in the context of science. Clearly, what is significant for one child is not necessarily for another. This is a welcome departure from the style of assessment which puts a set of arbitrary criteria, rather than the child's own development, as the basis of one's judgements. However, National Curriculum criteria are still considered, because the programmes of study have formed the basis of the planned learning intentions.

The more examples of significant achievement one sees, the clearer the idea becomes. If a child is a relatively slow learner, it does not mean that the child will have no significant achievement. It simply means that significance has to be redefined for that child. For instance, a child who takes six months to learn how to write her name will have a number of significant events leading up to the writing of the name (e.g. the first time she puts pen to paper, the first time she writes the initial letter of her name, etc). Similarly, a child who always does everything perfectly needs to be given more challenging, problem-solving activities in order to demonstrate significant achievement.

The *context* within which significant achievement can be spotted is usually the ongoing assessment dialogue, although it may be demonstrated by a product, such as a piece of writing the child has done. When significant achievements occur, they can be underplayed in a busy classroom. Children have the right to have *all* their significant achievements recognised, understood and recorded. Recognition consists of simply informing the child (e.g. 'Well done, that is the first time you have set your work out neatly').

Understanding *why* the significant event took place is a

crucial part of this process. It consists of asking the child *why* the significant achievement occurred. In trialling with teachers, we found that the child's answer often contradicts what the teacher saw as the reason for the significant achievement. This is an important discovery, because it shows that we must find out, from the child, why the significant achievement occurs if we are to be able to follow up the achievement with appropriate teaching strategies. One example of a piece of work brought to a course on significant achievement demonstrates the importance of finding out why the achievement took place:

6 *Ben chose for the first time to be a scribe in shared writing. Shared writing had been going on for over a year, with children in pairs, so this was significant for Ben. The teacher believed that this had happened because of the context of the story ('Horrible Red Riding Hood' – from the wolf's point of view), and her decision was to do more 'reverse' fairy stories as a way of encouraging Ben. However, when asked to go back and ask Ben why he had done this, the teacher reported that Ben said 'It was because you put me with Matthew, and he's shy, like me.' The implications for the teacher now are considerably different. Clearly Ben is sensitive to the dominance of the child he is working with, and the teacher's way forward now is to consider his pairing more carefully, both for writing and perhaps for other curriculum areas.* 9

The child should be central to the recognition and recording of the comment. During the course of a lesson, when the significant achievement occurs, the teacher, in a one-to-one situation, needs to make much of the event (e.g. *'Well done, Ben. This is the first time you have. . . . Tell me why this happened'*).

Models of recording significant achievement

In trialling this approach, we decided that any teacher records made should as far as possible be in the possession of the child, in order to have the most impact on the child's learning.

Two main types of achievement were identified: where it relates to a **product** (piece of work, drawing, etc) and where it relates to an **event**, with no accompanying work. The following list outlines the features of good, manageable, formative comments which would appear on the child's actual work, or, if it is an event with no product, on a separate piece of paper which is then slotted in to the child's Record of Achievement:

◆ the date
◆ *what* was significant
◆ *why* it was significant

An example of a comment for significant achievement:

❝ *Ben chose today, for the first time, to be the scribe in shared writing. This is a social skill and attitude development. Ben said he was able to do this because he was working with Matthew, who is quiet, like him.* ❞

A typical child's work would have traditional comments on most of the pages (e.g. *'Well done, Ben'*) and occasional comments *about* the child whenever significant achievement has occurred. The formative comment has many benefits:

◆ The child 'owns' the comment and has witnessed it being written, having been asked to say why the significant achievement took place.
◆ Parents and other interested parties find it much more meaningful to focus on the times when a significant formative comment has been written, because they make the progression of the child explicit.
◆ The child and teacher can look back to previous comments at any time, to compare with further progress and to help know what needs to be targetted for the future.

The Record of Achievement

The Record of Achievement is the place where any notable work is placed. The work should be negotiated between the teacher and the child. Unlike previous 'evidence collections', there is no systematic approach when using a Record of Achievement. It is simply an ongoing collection of any special work done by the child, and has been proved to be a highly motivating aspect of assessment. The Record can contain work or other measures of achievement from both inside and outside the school. Its main purpose is to motivate the child and impact on progress. Unlike the more traditional approach to Records of Achievement, the *teacher*, and not the child, is the main manager of the Record, negotiating with the child and gradually helping him/her to be able to identify significance for him/herself.

Summary

There are two places, then, where comments are written and placed when significant achievement takes place. **Written work or other products** have the comment written onto them and stay in the child's tray, or may be photocopied and placed in the child's Record of Achievement. **Event-style or non-product significant achievement** (e.g. organising a group of children) has the comment written on a piece of paper (often with a decorated border) which is then placed in the child's Record of Achievement. These records should be accessible to the child, not locked away and owned by the teacher. The ideal system is to have concertina folders in a box in the classroom.

Some teachers find that there are too many pieces of paper involved in *non-product* sheets, so prefer to record achievements in a single booklet for each child. This booklet is stored in the child's Record of Achievement and the child is simply asked to bring it to the teacher when something new is to be recorded in it. References to *product*-style achievements (e.g. *'See Danny's science work on 16 February'*) can also be made in this booklet or on separate sheets, so that there is then a one-to-one correspondence with all the significant achievements for a child and the number of references in the Record of Achievement. Keeping the comment in the child's exercise book or work without placing it in the Record of Achievement, however, has been found to be just as effective in motivating children. The most important thing is that children's achievements are explicitly recognised and a recording made.

In order to be able to easily access significant achievements in children's workbooks, some teachers place a coloured sticker in the top right-hand corner of the page where the comment had been made. This is not a 'praise' sticker, but simply a marker, which is very effective for being able to see progression quickly, and is especially useful for parents and writing reports.

The summative tracking system

So far, I have described the process of assessment and the accompanying formative record-keeping. However, so that the system is rigorous and children do not fall through the net, there needs to be some kind of summative tracking system. This should not be a burdensome task, so I suggest the following, simple mechanism: each half-term, term, or perhaps a whole year, the teacher takes an A3 sheet of centimetre-squared paper, or similar, and writes the children's names down the side and the contexts in which significant achievement might occur along the top. These would be, essentially, the teaching contexts. For example: Reading/Writing/Number/Shape and Space/Science topic/etc. The headings could also include the foundation subjects, but the statutory requirement is that records of some kind must be kept for the core subjects only. Bearing in mind our definition of significant achievement, however, it would seem appropriate to include all the teaching contexts, or perhaps have a further heading which simply says 'Other contexts'. A teacher in the early years would probably have different headings, such as Play/Role Play/Sand and Water/Constructional Play or Creative, Aesthetic, etc. Then, when significant achievement occurs, and the teacher has written the brief formative comment, she keeps track of this by entering the date and a code to show which category of significance occurred (see Figure 1).

This tracking record can serve a number of functions. At a glance the teacher may see:

◆ a few children who appear to have shown no significant achievement, and therefore need to be focused on, in case they have been missed because they are quiet;
◆ a child who has shown significant achievement in, say, reading, but not in writing, and who therefore needs to be checked;

Names	Speaking & listening	Reading	Writing	Number	Topic (Science etc.)	Other
Laura			8/2 Ⓒ		16/3 ⒶⒸ	4/2 ⒶⒸ
Cassie	3/3 ⓈⒶ	14/2 Ⓐ	19/3 Ⓒ	2/4 Ⓒ	1/2 ⓅⓈ	15/3 Ⓐ
Peter	4/2 ⒶⓈ	18/3 Ⓐ	21/2 ⒶⓅⓈ	1/3 ⒶⒸ	16/3 ⓅⓈ	3/4 ⓈⒶ
Roxanne		21/4 Ⓒ	21/4 ⓈⒶ	17/3 ⓅⓈ		
Sam	3/3 ⓅⓈ				17/3 Ⓒ	
Dean	12/1 Ⓐ	10/3 Ⓐ	28/3 ⒶⒸ	17/1 ⓅⓈ	11/3 Ⓟ	2/4 Ⓟ
Jenny	8/2 Ⓢ	8/2 ⒶⓅⓈ	4/1 Ⓒ	9/3 ⓅⓈ	20/3 Ⓒ	11/3 ⒶⓈ
Danny			18/3 Ⓒ		6/2 ⓅⓈ	9/3 ⒶⓈ

Ⓐ Attitude development   Ⓒ Conceptual development   Ⓟ Physical Skill
ⓅⓈ Process skill   Ⓢ Social skill

Figure 1

◆ the fact that none of the children has shown any significant achievement in, say, science, which indicates a need for the teacher to rethink the curriculum on offer;
◆ a bright child who appears to have shown no significant achievement, which indicates that he/she needs to be given more challenging, open-ended tasks.

One teacher in her second term of tracking significant achievement found that, on average, she recorded six comments per child in a half-term. Figure 2 shows some of these (these comments were written on the child's work or event sheet; and have only been reproduced in this way for the purpose of this book).

End-of-year records

Anything passed on to the next teacher needs to be useful to that teacher and able to be read quickly and easily. It is of no use passing on the whole Record of Achievement, because much of the content would have served its purpose

Yr 2 Name	Speaking / listening	Reading	Writing	Number	Topic	Other
Cassie	(S)(A) Took quite a complicated verbal message, and was able to deal with a query and bring back an answer.	(A) Is now choosing to read 'chapter' books.	(C) Writing consistently with correct sentence formation.	(C) Understanding concept of X and knows 2/5/10 tables – with understanding.	(PS) During experiment about light in relation to seeds. 'How can we water the ones that we have to keep covered?' (in the dark).	(A) Able to cope with 'not knowing' how to do something. She can now accept a challenge.
Peter	(A)(S) Co-operating with a partner to prepare for class assembly, and behaving in an appropriate manner during assembly.	(A) Avidly 'reads' books on the carpet, at the start of the school day.	(A)(P)(S) Sitting quietly and persevering with his improved handwriting.	(A)(C) Devising assorted maths problems with common answer (ways to make 8), he really persevered.	(PS) Seeds/light experiment. 'Put one lot of seeds up on the shelf – in the shade. (My Nan has a plant that doesn't get much light, it's in the hall.)'	(S)(A) Managing to play sociably with other children during playtime.
Dean	(A) Related own story, coherently, to ancillary.	(A) Enjoying using picture dictionaries to aid word recognition.	(A)(C) Can spell SPACE – verbally and written (other spelling very poor).	(PS) Was able to identify the need for string to aid measurement in a 'maze' problem.	(P) Made excellent – unaided – junk and clay models of a rhino.	(P) Persevering with learning to skip – he can do it!
Jenny	(S) Leading a small group discussion whilst making a group poster.	(A)(PS) Reading with good comprehension – completed task related to her reading.	(C) Use of common spelling patterns – what, which – who – when.	(PS) Independently solved 'maze' problem by using variety of measuring mediums – found that thread was easiest.	(C) Demonstrated reason for shadow disappearing/reappearing when body moves into a shadow.	(A)(S) Giving spontaneous praise to a child with low self-esteem.

Figure 2

and been surpassed by subsequent pieces of work. Good practice, therefore, is to sift the contents down to the last four pieces of significant work – say, one story, one account, one maths investigation and one science investigation. This will be manageable and useful for the next teacher to read. In the case of children with particular learning difficulties, it may be useful to pass on more pieces, perhaps showing the progression across the year.

As well as these pieces, the standard items passed on through the school would accompany them (e.g. reading record, end-of-year report, perhaps 'best fit' national curriculum levels for each child in the class). Teachers involved in trialling this system felt it unnecessary to pass on the summative tracking matrix, because this is essentially a working document.

Conclusion

This chapter outlines a framework for assessment which would first and foremost put the child's learning and development first. However, **this system can also meet the statutory requirements**. The following chapters have been carefully constructed to build on this chapter; giving examples of significant achievement, defining it within science itself, and answering the most common questions which teachers ask about looking for significant achievement.

Teachers, in trialling, were inspired and delighted by the fact that, at last, with this system, they could make the focus of their assessment practice the total development of the child, where **equal status is given to tiny steps, which might otherwise be seen as trivial, and more traditional demonstrations of progress**. The feedback has been, overall, that although it takes a while to get used to this different approach, the impact on the children's self-esteem and progress, the working atmosphere in the classroom, and children's ability to evaluate and set their own targets is considerable and, for some children, has resulted in leaps in progress which teachers have said would not otherwise have occurred. In their first summer after using tracking significant achievement, teachers said that their end-of-year records had never been easier to write.

It seems appropriate to end with some work from a child (Figure 3). The teacher asked the children, after their first term of focusing on significant achievement, to write a summary of their improvement. I believe that this child's account of his progress (and other accounts were all in the same vein) illustrates perfectly the emphasis that this philosophy places on the whole child, rather than just school-based learning.

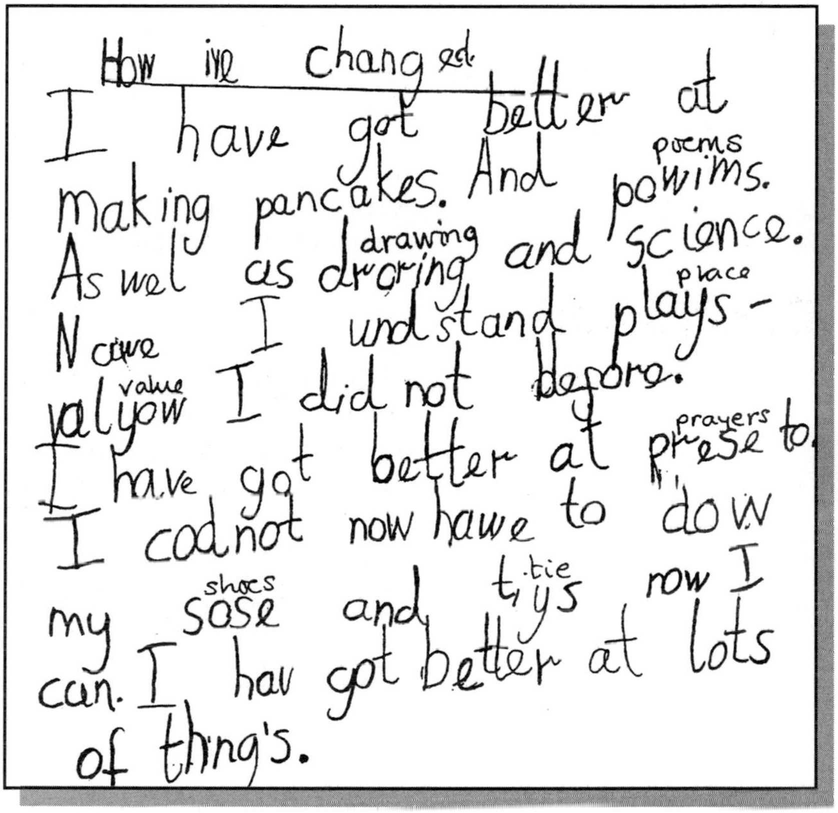

Figure 3

Reference

Drummond, M.J. (1993) *Assessing Children's Learning*, David Fulton Publishers.

2 Supporting Significant Achievement in Science

What do we mean by Science in the primary school?

From a young age children explore their immediate environment and begin to form ideas about the world around them. They recognise different kinds of birds in the park, they notice what happens when you mix cakes or cook eggs, or discover about water when they play in the bath. Science in the primary school seeks to build on these early experiences by helping children develop more effective, systematic ways of finding out and by providing opportunities for them to learn more about the biological and physical world. Primary science aims to:

◆ promote the development of **process skills** connected with scientific investigation, skills such as observing, questioning, predicting, hypothesising, investigating, interpreting, communicating and evaluating;

◆ extend children's **conceptual understanding** in relation to living things, materials, forces, energy and Earth in space;

◆ enhance children's **understanding of scientific procedures** - how to put together process skills and existing knowledge and understanding in tackling an investigation. This involves, for example, understanding how to set up a fair test or appreciating the need to consider the accuracy and range of measurements;

◆ encourage **scientific attitudes** such as curiosity, respect for evidence, critical reflection, flexibility and sensitivity to the living and non living environment, which influence children's development in science.

Although they can be discussed separately, it is important to recognise the links between concepts and processes in science. Scientific processes will be influenced by previous experience and ideas; conversely, process skills have an important role to play in concept development. To take an example from a Year 1 classroom:

❦ *Orange Class were exploring floating and sinking, making boats of different materials and trying them out in the water tray. Isabel made a paper boat just by folding up the sides of an A4 piece of paper and was delighted when it floated on the top of the water. She said 'I know it's going to float, it's light'. She then filled the bottom of the boat with plasticine and was astonished when it still floated. 'But it's too heavy', she explained. She tried adding some plastic farm animals and it still floated! Isabel was very puzzled by this unexpected result and kept pushing the boat as if to make it sink, saying 'it's too heavy'. For the rest of the week she kept going back to the water tray and trying her boat again.* ❧

Isabel's initial observations, and her prediction that her boat would sink, were influenced by her previous knowledge and experience of floating and sinking. At the same time she was using process skills such as observing and interpreting in modifying her original idea that light things float and heavy things sink.

As children progress through the primary school, it is important to encourage them to extend explorations such as the one described above into full investigations. Isabel could, for example, start to find out if the weight of an object affects whether it floats or sinks by testing objects of the same shape and material but different weights in the water tray. In carrying out and reviewing investigations, children can begin to develop their understanding of scientific procedures – for example, how and why you set up a fair test or why you need to take measurements several times.

What do we know about learning science?

In recent years two particular themes have emerged in studies of learning science: children's ideas and the role of practical work in science.

Children's ideas

Research since the 1970s suggests not only that children begin to develop ideas from a young age, but also that these ideas may be strongly held and often conflict with scientific thinking (as do the ideas of some adults!). Two examples may help to illustrate these and other general features of children's ideas.

Example 1: *Why do we get day and night?*

At the start of their project on Earth in Space Zaheer asked his Year 3 class why they thought we have day and night. Here are some of the answers they gave:

'The Sun goes behind the flats every night.'
'We have to have night time so we can go to sleep and have a rest.'
'The Earth goes round the Sun every day.'
'The Sun hides under the clouds.'

These explanations differ from the scientific explanation but, in common with many children's ideas, they do draw on observations from experience, even if they don't fit all the evidence.

Example 2: *What is an animal?*

Camilla divided her Year 4 class into groups of four and gave each group a set of cards showing pictures of a horse, a person, a cat, a butterfly, a worm, a stickleback, a bird, a frog, a dolphin, a tree and a daisy. She asked the children to sort the pictures into those that were animals and those that were not. She gave each group a chance to share and explain their decisions. Some of the comments in the feedback were as follows:

'It's rude to say someone's an animal. People aren't animals.'
'A butterfly isn't an animal, it's an insect.'

'A cat is an animal. It's furry and it's got four legs.'
'A worm isn't an animal. It hasn't got legs'.

The children's responses convey a narrow definition of an animal, perhaps something with legs or a mammal. They also hint at a common and important influence on children's ideas – everyday use of language. In a number of areas there are significant differences between everyday and scientific use of language – something children need to begin to appreciate.

There are some other characteristics worth mentioning. Children do not necessarily see the need for consistency: they may well give different explanations in different contexts or only take partial account of the evidence. Often they *describe* rather than *explain* events. However, most importantly, research has revealed there are common patterns of ideas in particular concept areas.

Current thinking about learning science gives widespread support for a 'constructivist' model for concept development. Key elements in this view of learning are:

◆ As children are likely to have developed their own ideas by the time they come to school (ideas which may be strongly held and in conflict with current scientific thinking), learning science will not just involve taking on new knowledge. It may require changing or *restructuring* current thinking. As a result learning science needs to be an *active* process whereby children use and test their ideas in new situations.
◆ It is important to acknowledge that social factors play a key role in learning. Children's ideas are influenced by the language and culture surrounding them.
◆ Many scientific ideas and explanations are unlikely to be *discovered* by children. Indeed, some scientific ideas seem to go against common sense – like the idea that heavy things can float or fly through the air. As a result, children will need to be introduced explicitly to the concepts and models of conventional science. They will then need support to make sense of these ideas for themselves and to apply them in appropriate situations.

The role of practical work in science

Historically, practical work has played a key role in primary science. The emphasis has been on activity and on first-hand experience. More recently teachers have begun to recognise that there are different kinds of practical work in science which may serve different purposes. Practical work in science can be divided into four basic types: *basic skills, observations, illustrations* and *investigations*.

Basic skills activities can help children develop particular skills or techniques they may need to use in their investigations – *for example, before testing parachutes you might want to make sure children know how to use a stopwatch or how to draw a graph from their results.*

Observations encourage children to observe in a scientific way. Children may be given a range of objects or events to describe, sort or classify, asked to relate observations to what they already know and identify relevant and important features. Observations often stimulate questions, predictions or hypotheses that could act as starting points for investigations – *for example, children might examine the rubbish they collected in the park and sort it into different groups.*

Illustrations are intended to illustrate a concept or a process. The idea is that children should experience and appreciate the key skill or concept without having to focus attention on decisions about apparatus or procedures. As a result, illustrations usually have recipe-like instructions that indicate what children should do – *for example, how to find out which materials dissolve in water.*

Investigations aim to give children opportunities to carry out their own investigations, to help them apply and develop their existing understanding of scientific concepts and procedures. Investigations in particular will support the development of procedural understanding and process skills. *Possible starting points for investigations will be questions which can be answered from first-hand data such as: Do bigger parachutes fall faster? What makes things go rusty?*

All types of practical work have important but different roles to play in learning science. What is vital is that teachers are clear about the purposes of different kinds of practical activity and about their own learning objectives in any particular task. Finally, there are a number of other key messages from recent studies of practical work in the classroom:

◆ We need to pay more attention to investigations. Currently most of the activities carried out in Key Stage 1 are observations and most at Key Stage 2 illustrations.
◆ Some aspects of investigations are frequently neglected: measurement, and more especially analysing and interpreting data and drawing conclusions at the end of investigations.
◆ Developing process skills and an understanding of scientific procedures cannot be left to chance and will not just happen through practising investigations. There is a need for explicit teaching and discussion.

Interactive approach to learning

Two opposing ways of teaching science have often been presented in the past: leaving children to discover for themselves or telling them the answers. Both are too simplistic. Children need to make sense of scientific ideas and come to grips with scientific procedures for themselves, but the teacher has a vital role in this process. Teachers can help children build confidence in themselves as learners, encouraging children to talk about their ideas, review how they carry out investigations, debate what their results mean and reflect on what they have learnt. This implies a different balance between practical activity and discussion than has been common in the past, with more time given to discussion and reflection.

Planning and organising science in the classroom

This suggests, first, that in planning science activities teachers need to find ways to build on children's ideas, provide opportunities for developing process skills and procedural understanding, and consider strategies for promoting scientific attitudes. Second, it indicates new and important roles for the teacher: being explicit about what learning science involves, listening to children's ideas and encouraging reflection on learning.

Building on children's ideas

Finding out children's ideas will be important at all stages in the planning process, from discussing the plan for the following year/term with the class to sharing thoughts at the start of a specific activity. The more difficult task for the teacher is learning how to build on the ideas that the children bring to the topic. The approach described below is based on the work of the Science Processes and Concept Exploration Project (described in Harlen 1992).

Exploration: Start by planning introductory activities that will give children a chance to think about their previous experience in your area of study. This helps children to orientate themselves to the new topic and provides you with opportunities to make a note of process skills or attitudes that need particular attention.

Finding out ideas: A variety of strategies can then be used to find out children's ideas. What is important is to give time and opportunity to make ideas explicit and to share and consider differing views.

Reflecting: Taking time to look at the children's responses is very worthwhile. Although you may have anticipated many of their ideas, this will help you to identify areas of particular difficulty and plan learning experiences to challenge and develop their thinking.

Helping children to develop their ideas and process skills: The kinds of activities planned will depend on the area of study. They could involve giving children a chance to test out their ideas; providing a range of illustrative tasks to challenge ideas or extend experience; encouraging children to apply ideas or procedures in a new situation; or sorting or discussion activities that enable them to talk about the meaning of particular words they use. Sometimes you may use second-hand sources or role play. There may be process skills you want to develop through practical exercises or discussion.

Assessing changes in ideas and process skills: Finally, both teacher and children need time to review changes in thinking or in process skills, and opportunities to apply their learning in new situations.

Developing process skills and procedural understanding

If children are to develop process skills and procedural understanding, they need a variety of practical experiences and appropriate support from the teacher. It is useful to review what has been planned for the term/year in science and consider: Is there a balance of different types of practical work? Will there be opportunities for children to develop the *full* range of process skills and to carry out their own investigations?

Some of the strategies teachers have found useful in supporting investigations are:

◆ planning jointly as a class, modelling how to set up an investigation, then providing opportunities for children to carry out similar investigations of their own;
◆ drawing up a checklist of questions to help children plan/review their investigations, for example *What do you predict and why?, How will you make your test fair?*
◆ having questions/suggestions books or noticeboards where children can put up their ideas; identifying a question for the week; using these to encourage children to suggest ideas for investigations;
◆ asking questions during an investigation: *Can you tell me what you are trying to find out?, How are you making it fair?, How are you going to measure?;*
◆ encouraging children to review and evaluate each other's investigations: *Was their test fair?, How accurate were their measurements?, Do the results support their conclusions?, What improvements would you suggest?*
◆ discussing the results and methods of recording of different groups: *Do the results agree?, Can you see any common patterns?, Which method worked best and why? , Do the results support their initial ideas?*
◆ giving children details of other people's investigations to analyse: *Were their tests fair?, What do their results show?*
◆ teaching children how to use tables, graphs or measuring instruments, discussing ideas of accuracy and the need to repeat measurements.

Promoting scientific attitudes

There are a number of ways in which teachers can foster scientific attitudes:

◆ Providing a stimulating environment, exciting materials and real first-hand experiences, valuing children's ideas and questions will be vital in fostering *curiosity*. Suggesting what you could look at or try out, spending time exploring alongside the children or showing a questioning approach yourself, can help promote interest and involvement.

◆ Encouraging children to discuss and draw up guidelines for care of living things or for safety in carrying out investigations will begin to develop an understanding of the need for *sensitivity to living things and the environment*. Praising children who work safely or discussing environmental issues will highlight this as an area of concern.

◆ Creating an atmosphere of trust and respect will be necessary if children are to be prepared to *respect evidence*, show *flexibility*, or *reflect critically* on their work. It will be important to plan opportunities to discuss alternative ideas and consider how methods could be improved. Sharing how your ideas have changed, emphasising that it doesn't matter if you are proved wrong, will be helpful in encouraging flexibility.

Being explicit about what learning science involves

Children may have very different ideas from the teacher about the nature and purposes of science activities and be unprepared for the challenge that learning science involves. Science in the primary school is concerned with developing and testing ideas and making sense of scientists' explanations and ways of proceeding. It is likely to involve making mistakes. It may even mean coming to grips with exciting and strange ideas that seem to go against common sense. Discussing views of science explicitly can help children take part more readily in this kind of process.

Providing opportunities for reflecting on learning

If children have talked about their ideas and plans at the start of a project, they will then be in a good position to reflect on their learning or the methods they used. It can be useful to plan a particular review session with the class, to go back to learning objectives and children's initial thoughts and consider, for example: *What have we found out?*, *How*

*have our ideas changed?, Could we improve on our
investigations/methods?, What further questions have we now?*
In this way, children and teacher share a sense of class
progress and are involved jointly in deciding next steps.

Listening to children's ideas

Many teachers who have been involved in projects or
courses looking at children's ideas have reported that they
now spend much more time *listening*. If pupils are to offer
their thoughts in discussion, all contributions must be
valued. Listening and acting as a neutral chair is a useful
strategy for the teacher, trying to allow the children to argue
with each other, rather than always intervening. Having
time when children do not have to compete with each
other, when each has a turn to speak, can give opportunities
for all children to express their ideas.

If children are to take an active part in discussion, they need
time to think through their responses and to find the words
to express their ideas. If teachers wait just a few extra
seconds after asking a question, pupils' responses tend to be
longer and more confident and more children are likely to
participate.

Creating a climate for learning science

Classroom atmosphere

To be successful learners, children need positive images of
themselves, and to feel safe and secure. The following
strategies can support the development of a positive
classroom atmosphere:

Promoting equal opportunities: A concern for equality will
influence all aspects of classroom life – resources, groupings,
methods of assessment, etc. In particular, in science, taking
into account the differing interests and experiences of boys
and girls will be important. Children may make negative
comments or have already absorbed racist, sexist or other
stereotyped attitudes. It is vital to challenge such comments
and to foster children's respect for each other and the
contributions they all make to school life. Science has an

important role in extending children's understanding of the world and in challenging prejudice.

Building on children's home experiences: Children's earliest learning takes place in their home and community. Recognising and valuing this early experience can promote continuity of learning and help children to feel confident in school.

Having high expectations and valuing the contributions of all children: To develop a sense of self-esteem, children need to be shown that their unique contributions are valued and that their efforts, ideas and work are appreciated. It is vital to ensure that the work of *all* children is shared and displayed, and that all have a chance to put forward their ideas.

Encouraging children to learn from their mistakes: Frequently mistakes or unexpected results are very effective in promoting learning in science. Often it is just as important to know what *doesn't* work as what does. For example, finding all the circuits that *don't* work can help children to appreciate the importance of a complete circuit. If children do it right the first time, they may not know why and learn less!

Helping children to develop a sense of their own progress: Children are likely to be much more motivated if they have a picture of their own progress. This can be encouraged in a number of ways, including:

◆ displaying examples of new achievements;
◆ recording achievements in pupils' profiles or records of achievement;
◆ telling them what you have noticed (for example: *'You worked really well with Andreas or remembered to use the same amount of water to make it a fair test'*);
◆ having a special class time for children to share things they are proud of;
◆ reviewing what the class has gained at the end of an activity or project;
◆ asking children what they think about how they are doing in science;
◆ talking with the children while you are marking work;
◆ asking children to evaluate their own work;
◆ encouraging children to engage in peer evaluation.

Supporting collaborative learning: A classroom in which children listen to each other and are supportive and cooperative will also enable children to learn from each other. Some children may need support and encouragement to collaborate. It is often necessary to monitor groups carefully and to use different groupings at different times to ensure particular individuals are not dominating activities.

Classroom organisation and resources

Providing a stimulating environment and organising the classroom to support independence can both be important in promoting learning in science.

An important part of the teacher's role in science is in planning and organising classroom resources. A classroom that *looks* interesting and inviting can help to stimulate curiosity and eagerness to learn. Interactive displays of materials or living things allow children to become familiar with them, to go back and look again and repeat investigations. Leaving equipment out enables the less confident to go and try an activity once the rush is over, and experiment with new ideas. Science reference books, posters and displays can also stimulate science questions and investigations.

Having resources readily available can help children plan and equip their own investigations. Organising space so that there are a variety of areas where children can work together, talk and share ideas helps to promote reliance on each other. If the children are finding it difficult to work independently and are over-reliant on the teacher, it is worth keeping a record of interruptions and then sharing this with the class. Often the results indicate particular difficulties with resources, lack of understanding of the task or just general needs for reassurance. Sometimes changes in organisation or new ways of presenting tasks can help children work more effectively on their own. Discussing problems with the children can often produce useful ideas for improvements.

Context for learning

Young children learn best in a context that is familiar and has meaning for them. Building on children's previous experiences, starting from their ideas and setting science activities in the context of their immediate environment, can help create interest and give meaning to science activities.

Ensuring children understand the purpose of science activities: If children are to take part effectively in activities and evaluate their own progress, it is important to make sure they understand the *purpose* of the task they are undertaking. At the start of a project it is useful to draw up learning objectives and list outline plans with the class. Sometimes plans will be modified by the children's responses, and it enables children to see the overall direction of the work. The learning objectives for particular activities can be shared in a number of ways:

◆ talking about objectives at the start, for example: *'I'm looking to see how safe you can be in doing this heating experiment'* or *'We've been talking about measuring, so think about being as accurate as you can and make sure you check your measurements'*;
◆ listing main objectives on the board – it could just be one word: *safety, measuring, what affects how fast the parachutes fall*;
◆ talking with children during the activities to draw out your objectives: *'How are you making this safe?'*, *'What ideas have you come up with so far about the parachutes?'*;
◆ stopping the class periodically to share good ideas and remind them of the main focus of the work;
◆ reviewing the task at the end as a whole class, sharing successes, useful strategies and ideas;
◆ encouraging children to assess their own progress and those of their friends.

Differentiating activities: For children to progress, work needs to be appropriately differentiated to take account of their differing needs and aptitudes. To feel motivated and confident, children need to experience both challenge and success. There are many ways of building in differentiation, both in advance and as an activity progresses. Here are some examples:

◆ providing different activities;
◆ presenting activities in different ways – discussion, demonstration, written instructions, giving a general introduction to the whole class and then further individual attention to groups/individuals to get them going;
◆ varying the number of decisions children have to make about equipment, measuring, constructing a fair test or recording, so some children make fewer decisions;
◆ arranging extra support for some children, further instructions, use of computer or tape, translating key words or instructions, providing a visual display, using support staff;
◆ planning extension activities or giving extra consolidation experiences;
◆ giving differing amounts of time to the activity;
◆ encouraging children to record in different ways;
◆ arranging different groupings.

Finally, in considering a project overall, it is important to provide a range of different types of learning experience – practical activity, discussion, use of reference material, drama, computers, etc, as different children prefer to learn in different ways. In this way you are ensuring that some parts of what you do will coincide with each child's learning style.

Significant achievement in science

Having discussed how you might try to provide a positive climate for learning science, in what ways do children develop, and what might significant achievement look like? The answer will very much depend on the individual child. However, as suggested in Chapter 1, experience indicates that significant achievement can fall into a number of categories: *physical skill, social skill, attitude development, concept clicking* or *process skill*. For example:

◆ Many science activities involve handling tools or equipment such as saws or scissors or sellotape. This may indicate the development of **physical skills**.
◆ Often tasks require cooperation with others and may reveal **social skills**.

◆ With young children, just beginning to show an interest in scientific activity or being prepared to talk about their experiences may be important steps forward indicating **attitude development.**

◆ Over a period of time you may notice changes in approach to investigations such as the recognition of: the need for a fair test, the importance of measurement or the need to consider how far the evidence supports the conclusions made, suggesting development in **process skills.**

◆ The children may draw together a range of experiences to develop their understanding of a new concept, suggesting **concept clicking.** Often the questions children ask tell you a great deal about their knowledge and understanding.

It is these general trends, the development of new skills or changes in underlying attitudes or characteristics of thinking, rather than isolated aspects of knowledge or behaviour, that help to identify significant achievement. How might you identify change or development? It is possible to map out some useful features of development, but experience suggests that there are no set paths or stages. Children may come to the same point in many different ways, and their progress may be uneven.

Attitude development

Here it is important to distinguish between *attitudes to science* (for example whether children like science, what they feel about scientists or scientific activity) and *scientific attitudes*. Some general features of development in scientific attitudes are shown below:

Area	FROM ...	TO ...
Curiosity	... being unaware of new things and showing little interest.	... noticing details; seeking for explanations.
Respect for evidence	... reporting results that are in line with their original ideas, ignoring conflicting evidence.	... drawing conclusions from the evidence, recognising the tentative nature of conclusions.

Critical reflection	. . . needing encouragement to review methods, findings or ideas.	. . . reviewing and evaluating independently, suggesting ideas for change and improvement.
Flexibility	. . . tending to stick to preconceived ideas.	. . . considering other points of view, being prepared to change ideas.
Sensitivity to living and non-living environment	. . . needing supervision to show appropriate concern and responsibility.	. . . showing awareness of the needs of living things, aware of the importance of respecting the environment.

Children may also show changes in attitudes *to* science, for example from being reluctant to take part in science activities to participating willingly, from fear and dislike to enjoyment.

Development in process skills

Children's process skills and their performance in investigations will be very much dependent on the context and the concepts involved and their previous experience, knowledge and understanding. Progression will be shown by an increasingly systematic approach. The following table indicates some general trends in the development of process skills:

Area	**FROM . . .**	**TO . . .**
Observing	. . . observing obvious details and differences.	. . . noting patterns in observations relevant to problem.
Raising questions	. . . readily asking questions, often not in a form that can be investigated.	. . . formulating questions that can be investigated.

Area	FROM ...	TO ...
Predicting	... being prepared to make a prediction, often based on partial evidence.	... making predictions using patterns in data, showing how evidence has been used.
Hypothesising	... offering explanations based on everyday experience.	... offering explanations based on scientific knowledge and theories, showing an awareness of their tentative nature, suggesting ways of checking.
Investigating	planning as you go along; beginning to recognise the need for a fair test; using simple qualitative variables; using basic measuring techniques.	adopting a systematic approach; identifying and measuring key variables in a fair test; using measuring equipment; considering range and accuracy of measurements.
Interpreting	... describing simple relationships.	... identifying patterns in data; evaluating data in relation to original problem.
Communicating	... using simple techniques, drawing, writing usually after an	... using more formal and more systematic methods, appropriate for investigation. the audience and purpose; recording during and accurate reporting after an investigation.

Conceptual development

Here it is worth making a distinction between *content* and *concepts* in science.

Content is the subject matter of an area of study, for example seeing what happens when you mix salt or sugar with water, or observing and studying the minibeasts in leaf litter. **Concepts** are overall ideas or generalisations that children may develop through these activities that will apply to a much wider range of situations. In this case the activities might help to develop concepts such as dissolving, habitat or food chain.

Concepts are unlikely to develop as the result of just one experience. Children will need to come across ideas and have opportunities to apply them in a range of contexts. Harlen & Jelly (1989) identify two strands in the development of concepts: *range* and *degree of abstraction*.

Aspect	FROM ...	TO ...
Range	... expressing ideas that relate to one situation.	... making links between different situations, using the same idea to explain a range of experiences.
Degree of abstraction	... describing observations.	... generalising about relationships, using models, relating concepts to more abstract qualities.

For example, children may progress:

FROM being able to describe how to make their bulb light
TO the recognition of the need for a complete circuit;

FROM being able to describe what they do to look after their pet
TO understanding the needs for life.

This kind of development is hinted at in the National Curriculum (DFE 1995), where an examination of the level descriptions suggests the following pattern of development:

◆ observing, discussing using everyday language;
◆ noting similarities and differences, recognising simple relationships;
◆ classifying phenomena, linking cause and effect, offering reasons;
◆ explaining, using scientific vocabulary;
◆ using abstract ideas, models, generalising across contexts, applying ideas.

However, as with process skills, it is vital not to see these as definite stages or as indicators of a linear model of development.

How can significant achievement be promoted?

Some features of the approach to teaching and learning described in this chapter are particularly important in promoting significant achievement:

◆ a programme that builds on children's previous experience and ideas;
◆ a broad range of experiences that will enable development of skills, attitudes, knowledge and understanding in science;
◆ a variety of teaching and learning approaches which promote children's active involvement in their own learning, encourage children to make their own decisions and suggest their own ideas;
◆ discussion about what learning science involves;
◆ a recognition that making mistakes and changing ideas is an inevitable and important part of learning science;
◆ clarification of the learning objectives of each activity;
◆ a classroom climate which encourages risk-taking and supports independence;
◆ opportunities to reflect on learning;
◆ dialogue between pupil and teacher to share factors that have helped promote learning and identify new goals.

Further examples of factors that help to promote significant achievement emerge in Chapter 3, where we look at practical examples of significant achievement in the classroom.

Further reading

General reading on primary science

Association for Science Education (ASE) *Primary Science Review* (primary science journal of ASE, produced five times a year).

Browne, N. (Ed) (1991) *Science and Technology in the Early Years*, Open University Press (addresses gender issues).

Department for Education (1995) *Science in the National Curriculum*, HMSO.

Harlen, W. (1985) *Primary Science: Taking the Plunge*, Heinemann Educational.

Harlen, W. and Jelly, S. (1989) *Developing Science in the Primary Classroom*, Oliver and Boyd.

Harlen, W. (1992) *The Teaching of Science*, David Fulton.

Harlen, W. (1993) *Teaching and Learning Primary Science* (second edition), Paul Chapman.

NCC (1989) *Science Non-Statutory Guidance*, National Curriculum Council.

NCC (1993) *Teaching Science at Key Stages 1 and 2*, National Curriculum Council.

Peacock, A. (Ed.) (1991) *Science in Primary Schools: The Multicultural Dimension*, Macmillan Education.

Sherrington, R. (1993) *ASE Primary Science Teachers' Handbook*, Simon and Schuster.

Thorp, S., Deshpande, P. & Edwards, E. (Eds) (1994) *Race, Equality and Science Teaching*, ASE.

Children's ideas in science

Driver, R. (1983) *The Pupil as Scientist*, Open University Press.

Driver, R., Guesne, E. and Tiberghien, A. (1985) *Children's Ideas in Science*, Open University Press.

Nuffield Primary Science (1993, revised 1995) *Teachers' Handbooks for Key Stages 1 and 2*, Collins.

Primary SPACE project reports (1990 onwards) *Evaporation and Condensation, Growth, Light, Sound, Electricity, Materials, Rocks, Soils and Weather, Processes of Life* – some reports still to be published, Liverpool University Press.

Osborne, R. and Freyberg, P. (1985) *Learning in Science*, Heinemann Educational.

Investigations and process skills in primary science

Galton, M. and Harlen, W. (series eds) (1990) *Assessing Science in the Primary Classroom: Written Tasks, Practical Tasks, Observing Activities* (three books), Paul Chapman Publishing.

Goldsworthy, A. and Feasey, R. (1994) *Making Sense of Primary Science Investigations*, ASE.

Johnsey, R. (1992) *Primary Science Investigations*, Simon and Schuster.

3 Significant Achievement in the Classroom

The previous chapters have considered planning for significant achievement and ways to identify and promote significant achievement in science. This chapter aims to draw this all together by showing you concrete examples of significant achievement in science from a wide range of different classrooms. By the end of this chapter you will start to have a real sense of what significant achievement might look like in science and feel confident you can begin to recognise it in your own classroom.

The examples of significant achievement shown in this chapter are drawn from across the primary age range. They were not produced in exceptional circumstances. They come from everyday classrooms with children of different backgrounds and abilities. Nor do they necessarily show outstanding pieces of work. They are special, however, because in each case the teacher has noticed a significant new step in the child's scientific development. The examples illustrate the range of different types of significant achievement discussed in Chapter 1 and highlight many of the factors that often contribute to significant achievement outlined in Chapter 2.

Each example starts by giving a description of what happened. In many cases the child's recording is shown which indicates some aspects of the child's response. However, it is important to note that often it is not the child's records, but the teacher's observations of what the child said or did, that are vital in identifying significant achievement. This is followed by four important pieces of information:

Why was this significant? – why this event was significant for *this* child.

Why did it happen? – the child's view of why it happened, and in some cases factors that in the teacher's view may have prompted significant achievement.

Type of significant achievement – physical skill, social skill, attitude development, process skill or concept clicking.

Comment – ways forward for the child and any general implications for practice.

The examples are organised into three sections corresponding to the major content areas of science in the National Curriculum: Life and Living Processes, Materials and their Properties, and Physical Processes. Each section starts with the youngest children and contains a variety of types of significant achievement.

Life and Living Processes

Mohameed (Year 1): *Worms*

The class were about to take part in a worm hunt to find worms for a new nature garden being established in the local area. The children were asked to write down any questions they had about worms. These would form the basis for further investigations in school. Mohameed wrote:

> 6 *I am a warm sitsest [scientist] on a prot [project] on warms. I wont to no if warms torn into butterflis. if catepillrs are the same as warms.* 9

Why was this significant?

Mohameed very rarely came up with questions. Here he put forward a question about the life cycle of a worm that suggests he was making links with past experiences of keeping caterpillars in the classroom.

Why did it happen?

Mohameed said he was very excited about finding worms and keeping them in the classroom: *'I want to know if they have babies.'*

Type: **process skill** (questioning)

Comment

The prospect of keeping living things in the classroom stimulated Mohameed's curiosity. The combination of this exciting experience with the teacher's focus on raising questions for investigation helped prompt Mohameed's question.

Living things in the classroom almost always prompt lots of questions. Recording and working from these questions very much helps encourage interest and involvement. Questions often reveal the way children are making sense of a new area of study and the links they see with past experience.

Karim (Year 2): *Worms*

The children were finding out whether worms like dry or damp places by putting them between dry and damp soil and seeing which way they went. Karim offered his ideas about what worms prefer, based on his personal experience.

> I no that Worm's like the damp place's. and bicas in my gardan it rande and after a wille after a wille the rane stopt and the clod's went the growd was sgy I wnetid for a wille and then the Worms came up from there Barows and poct itched on of the hole.

Why was this significant?

Karim gave a very vivid description of what he had observed, including many relevant features that could be explored further.

Why did it happen?

Karim said he was interested in worms and had watched worms at home in his garden.

Type: process skill (observing and predicting)

Comment

Building on Karim's interest in living things and his home experiences will be important in future. Karim's prediction that worms like damp soil was tested out in the classroom investigations.

It would be possible for children to investigate whether you find more worms after rain or on a wet day. They could explore whether other minibeasts prefer damp places and suggest explanations for their findings.

Joe (Year 2): *Growing seeds*

The children were asked to think about what plants need to grow and to consider how they could test their ideas. They decided to see if plants need water and if they grow better in the dark or in the light. Joe suggested that plants need water *'because our ones at home need water'*. He offered an explanation about why the plants in the dark had grown taller: *'because it does not get jogged – my mum's bonsai plant does not like getting jogged. It upsets them.'*

Why was this significant?

Joe was able to put forward ideas clearly based on his past experience.

Why did it happen?

Joe said ' *I know because I grow plants at home.'*

Type: process skill (hypothesising which plants will grow better and why)

Comment

Joe could test out his ideas about why plants grow taller in the dark. He could begin to consider how he might set up a fair test and use measurement in his investigations.

This is a good example of the way in which building on previous experience enables children to offer their ideas, suggestions and explanations in investigations.

Jessie (Year 3): *Pulse rate*

The children tested their pulse rate before and after activity. Jessie measured and recorded her partner's pulse rate very carefully. She repeated measurements to check their accuracy. She noticed that exercise made her pulse rate increase.

Why was this significant?

Jessie took much greater care than usual in making and recording her measurements and decided to repeat measurements to check their accuracy.

Why did it happen?

Jessie said, *'It was exciting. Susan's pulse rate went up a lot. It surprised me, so I did it again.'*

Type: process skill (measuring – recognising the need to repeat measurements)

Comment

The teacher asked Jessie to share her results and her reasons for repeating measurements with the class. She emphasised that it is necessary to check results even if they are not surprising.

Children need to be encouraged to consider their emerging results, to identify patterns, puzzles and unexpected values. Often they write down results without noticing what is happening.

Sabrina (Year 3): *Making a model of a tree*

The children had been on a trip to the park and were recording their experiences in a variety of ways. Sabrina decided to make a 3-D model of a tree showing all the different animals she had found living on and around it. She succeeded in doing this all by herself.

Why was this significant?

Sabrina has poor fine motor control and has difficulty using scissors or manipulating small objects. She often gets frustrated and gives up.

Why did it happen?

Sabrina said, '*It was good at the park.*'

Type: physical skill (using scissors, making small objects such as models of minibeasts). The example also shows **attitude development** (perseverance).

Comment

Sabrina was so inspired by her visit to the park, she talked about nothing else all week. It will be important to take all possible opportunities to go out into the local environment in future.

First-hand experience in the local environment is very motivating. It often stimulates new developments in skills, attitudes or concepts.

Marc (Year 4): *Sound and hearing*

The children worked in groups of five to devise a way to investigate hearing. They developed their own methods of recording and were given a series of questions to help focus their reports.

Experiment on Sound

Things we need —
1) Metal pot
2) Dice
3) Chair
4) Blind fold
5) Pencil

Who was in our group —
1) Lucas
2) Nicole
3) Me (Marc)
4) Jan
5) Samara

We done this experiment to see who had the best hearing, which ear they can hear through best and if it is more easy to hear it being shaken with a dice inside or when it was being hit with a pencil. It was harder to know where it was coming from with the pencil more.

CHART TO SHOW HOW GOOD WE WERE	LEFT		RIGHT		FRONT		BEHIND	
	HIGH	LOW	HIGH	LOW	HIGH	LOW	HIGH	LOW
1) Nicole —7	X	✓	X	✓	✓	✓	✓	✓
2) Jan —7	✓	✓	✓	✓	X	X	X	X
3) Samara —7	✓	✓	✓	✓	✓	X	X	X
4) Marc —7	✓	X	X	X	✓	✓	X	✓
5) Lucas —7	✓	✓	✓	✓	✓	✓	✓	✓

What was significant?

Marc worked well within the group and was able to interpret his results.

<u>Results</u>

1) Lucas had the best 'hearing'

2) The left ear worked best for Most People

3) It was easier to hear in front than behind.

4) I noticed that the People who were tested with the Pencil move got less Points than People who were tested with the dice move, and because your left-handed it doesn't mean your left-eared.

BRILLIANT
Super work!

Why did it happen?

Marc said that they discussed in the group who should do what and what the results showed.

Type: process skill (interpreting results) and **social skill** (cooperation)

Comment

The teacher gave positive feedback to the group, congratulating them on how well they had worked together. This gave Marc important encouragement. For the future, it would be interesting to compare the methods and results of different groups, emphasising the importance of interpreting and evaluating results.

Sam (Year 6): *Muscles at work*

The children were given a series of activities to try: clenching your fingers, bending/straightening your arm, pressing down hard on a desk, and trying gently to lift a desk while your partner pressed down. In each case the children were asked if they could see or feel anything happening in their lower or upper arm. Sam showed an interest in finding out how his muscles worked and collaborated well with his group. He recognised that the human body *'needs to be treated with respect'*.

Why was this significant?

Sam normally finds it hard to work with others. Initially he had been reluctant to join the group or find out about the body. He said *'It's disgusting.'* On occasions he has treated other children roughly. His comments suggest he is beginning to think about the effect this has.

Why did it happen?

Sam said *'I was aware that if I lifted it up too much I could be injured . . . You know not to do the wrong thing because your arm can't take it.'* The practical experience seemed to have made quite an impact on him, both in arousing his interest and in encouraging him to reflect on his own behaviour.

Type: attitude development (showing care and responsibility towards himself and others and curiosity) and **social skills** (working with a group)

Comment

Sam could follow up this work by sharing his findings and their implications with the class or another group, and by reading some information books in this area. The teacher planned to encourage him to work further with the same group.

Erica (Year 6): *Living things in the environment*

Following work on minibeasts, the teacher used a task developed by the Children's Learning in Science Project (CLIS 1992) to explore children's ideas about relationships between living things in the environment. The teacher had prepared a large picture showing the Sun, the sky, ground and a stream, and cardboard cut-outs of a range of different plants and animals. The children were asked to select six living things that could live there for a long time, stick them on the picture and explain their choices. Erica chose a bird, a tree, a worm, a beetle, a squirrel and some dandelions. She said *'The squirrel can live in the tree and eat the nuts. The bird can live in the tree and it can eat worms or beetles. Beetles eat worms too and the worms live in the dirt and eat leaves. But you need two squirrels and two birds so they have babies.'*

Why was this significant?

Erica indicated an awareness that animals would need to find food and shelter and need to reproduce.

Why did it happen?

Later Erica said ' *When I was lost I would need food and somewhere to sleep.'*

Type: concept clicking (animals' needs – food, shelter, reproduction)

Comment

The teacher had not used this task before and was surprised at how well the discussion went. It encouraged her to try out other strategies for eliciting ideas. She introduced the idea of a food chain and encouraged children to draw up as many food chains as they could from the animals provided. These were then recorded and links between the chains discussed to make a food web.

Many of the tasks and questions devised by the SPACE and CLIS projects are very useful in encouraging children to reveal their ideas and understanding (see page 43 for SPACE references).

CLIS (1992) *Progression in understanding of ecological concepts by pupils age 5 to 16*, University of Leeds.

Materials and their Properties

Melvin (Reception): *Making pancakes*

The class made pancakes for Shrove Tuesday. Melvin commented that the pancake mixture was *'bubbling on the oven'*. It went from *'soggy'* to *'hard and flat like a fried egg'*. He recorded what happened in sequence without help.

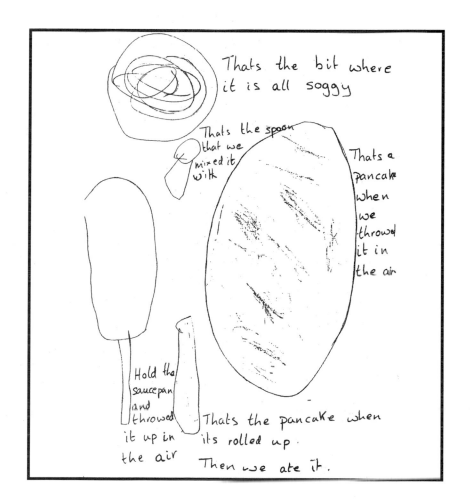

Thats the bit where it is all soggy

Thats the spoon that we mixed it with

Thats a pancake when we throwed it in the air

Hold the saucepan and throwed it up in the air

Thats the pancake when its rolled up. Then we ate it.

Why was this significant?

Melvin made a link with his past experience of cooking. He is beginning to notice a pattern in the way materials change when heated. He recorded the sequence of events independently. This is something he has never done before.

Why did it happen?

Melvin said he likes cooking: *'It felt yummy.'* Melvin was working on his own when he was recording: perhaps this helped him in producing work of a higher quality than before.

Type: concept clicking (patterns in changes that take place on heating). The example also shows **attitude development** (confidence and independence in recording) and **process skill** (observing, communicating).

Comment

Trying to find exciting contexts that relate to Melvin's interests and past experience is important. Melvin needs further experience of other changes that take place on heating, such as melting, burning. The teacher decided to observe whether he records better when working on his own.

Being able to make links with past experience, as Melvin did, is vital in the development of concepts. In planning activities, it is worth identifying the differing kinds of previous experience children may have had, and considering ways of encouraging children explicitly to discuss and make links with that experience.

Sally (Year 1): *How to stop food going bad*

Food was being bought to make sandwiches for the class bakery and the class needed to decide how to keep the food fresh. The children were asked to devise their own experiment to test how to stop food going bad. Sally understood you needed to *'test two of the same thing [bread] to make it fair'*. She tried to explain to the other children in her group that their tests were not fair.

Why was this significant?

Sally had not talked about the need for a fair test before.

Why did it happen?

Sally said she thought about *'when we tested how beans sprout'*. She seemed to be relating back to previous discussions in the class about fair testing.

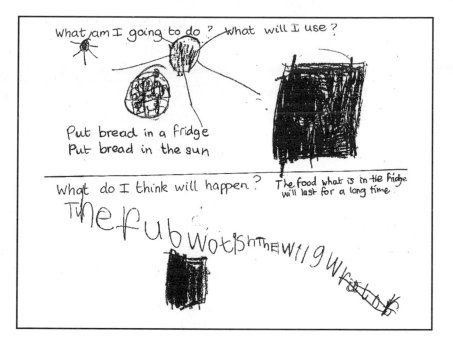

Type: process skill (fair testing)

Comment

It is worthwhile reminding children about previous experiences of fair testing when tackling new investigations. Sally needs further opportunities to devise her own tests, using and handling an increasing number of variables.

This is a good example of a child who was introduced to fair testing with the support of the teacher and is now able to devise a simple fair test on her own. Two elements are important in this process: first, the introduction of a particular process skill; second, opportunities to use and apply this skill in new situations (with the reminders of previous experience!).

Claire (Year 1): *Sorting materials*

The children were sorting different objects and materials and discussing how they felt to touch. The word 'rough' was introduced and used. Claire kept repeating the word 'rough' to herself as she found rough materials and objects. She was able to share what she had done in whole-class discussion on the carpet. She was very keen to talk about her new experience.

Why was this significant?

Claire learnt a new word, 'rough'. She had previously described anything rough as hard: she used the word 'hard' to describe everything rough even if the object was soft. This was also the first time Claire had spoken in front of the whole class. She was new to the class and was usually shy.

Why did it happen?

Being introduced to a new idea in a practical context and having opportunities to apply that new idea may have helped Claire to make this significant achievement. Claire was able to touch and describe what she felt. The word 'rough' was introduced. Then Claire had opportunities to use and find examples of the new word.

Type: concept clicking (concept 'rough' – distinguishing from 'hard'). It also shows **social skill**: confidence in speaking before the whole class.

Comment

Introducing new words in a practical context is valuable. Claire needs further opportunities to explore, test and sort materials, and encouragement to share her findings with the class.

In science it is often important to help children develop more specific definitions for words they use, and to extend their vocabulary. Exploration of the properties of materials may lead, for example, to discussion of the difference between hard, strong and heavy or the introduction of new words such as flexible, brittle, opaque. The children can be asked to make collections of objects to illustrate these words, helping them to define the words through using them in a practical context.

Andrea (Year 2): *Making jelly*

The class discussed what would happen when you put jelly in hot water, warm water and cold water. They talked about what they thought would happen, tested it out and recorded their results. Andrea recorded her findings confidently.

Why was this significant?

Andrea is normally very reluctant to record at all.

Why did it happen?

Andrea said '*I like jelly.*' The teacher had provided a structure for recording, breaking down the page into sections, that may have encouraged Andrea to contribute.

Type: process skill (recording); the example also shows **attitude development** (confidence and interest in recording).

Comment

Building on Andrea's interests may help her to apply herself more readily to science activities. It will be important to explore and discuss with Andrea different ways of recording, including ways of structuring her work.

Often children are daunted by a blank page for recording. They are not sure what to do and may feel that what you expect is a page of writing. Providing prompt questions, discussing different ways of recording, or just dividing a sheet into a few sections can help encourage children to record.

Note: Children often confuse 'melting' and 'dissolving'.

Abdul (Year 4): *Insulation*

The class had been discussing insulation. Abdul set up an investigation to find out if insulating materials always made things hotter. He noticed that a jumper kept the hot water hotter but it also kept the cold water colder. He offered an explanation for his findings.

Why was this significant?

Abdul changed his ideas. He recognised that the jumper did not warm the cold water up, it actually kept it cool. Furthermore, he did not just describe his findings, he attempted to offer an explanation based on his ideas about air being trapped in the holes in the jumper.

Why did it happen?

Abdul said *'It didn't turn out like I expected. It made me think.'*

Type: **attitude development** (flexibility in changing ideas, respect for evidence). The example also shows **process skill** (offering an explanation) and **concept clicking** (insulating material can slow down heating/cooling).

Comment

This example illustrates the way in which allowing children to test out their ideas can help them to change and develop their thinking (as suggested in Chapter 2). Unexpected results play a particularly important role in learning.

Abdul has recognised that insulating material can help keep things hot or cool. He could now be encouraged to measure and think about the temperature difference between the cup of water and its surroundings, and to discuss what would happen if the insulating material was removed, and why.

Ian (Year 5): *Drying soils*

Ian planned an investigation to find out whether soil would dry out more slowly if kept in a plastic bag. He recognised that he had not carried out a fair test because he had used different amounts of soil. He offered an explanation for his findings (see over).

Why was this significant?

Ian thought carefully about whether he had carried out a fair test. He had clear ideas about what had happened in his investigation.

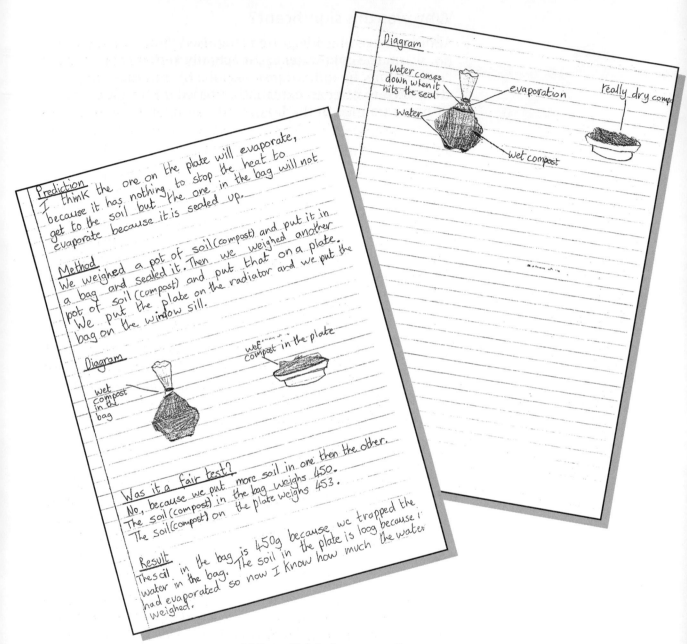

Diagram

Water comes down when it hits the seal

evaporation

really dry comp

water

wet compost

Prediction

I think the one on the plate will evaporate, because it has nothing to stop the heat to get to the soil but the one in the bag will not evaporate because it is sealed up.

Method

We weighed a pot of soil (compost) and put it in a bag and sealed it. Then we weighed another pot of soil (compost) and put that on a plate. We put the plate on the radiator and we put the bag on the window sill.

Diagram

wet compost in the plate

wet compost in the bag

Was it a fair test?

No, because we put more soil in one then the other. The soil (compost) in the bag weighs 450. The soil (compost) on the plate weighs 453.

Result

The soil in the bag is 450g because we trapped the water in the bag. The soil in the plate is 100g because I had evaporated so now I know how much the water weighed.

Why did it happen?

Ian said the teacher had asked him to think about his test and his results.

Type: attitude development (critical reflection); the example also shows **process skill** (fair testing and interpreting results).

Comment

Although Ian had recognised that using different amounts of soil made his test unfair, he had not realised that putting the two pots of soil in different parts of the classroom, on the window sill and on the radiator, was also a problem. The teacher decided to discuss the variables involved in this investigation further with the class, emphasising that there might be a number of variables they would need to consider.

Teacher prompts can be useful in encouraging children to focus on key aspects of investigations. However, if children have not grasped fully the idea of a fair test, just asking them to think about this will not be enough! Further discussion and teaching will be necessary.

Andrew (Year 5): *Which cream would make the most butter?*

Andrew carried out an investigation to find out which kind of cream would make the most butter. He wrote *'The double cream will make the most butter because the double cream has got more fat than the whipping cream.'* His results were consistent with his hypothesis (see over).

Why was this significant?

Andrew used his previous knowledge and experience of making butter in formulating his hypothesis. In the past he had been prepared to make suggestions about what would happen, but rarely offered an explanation for his ideas.

Why did it happen?

Andrew said *'I remembered when we made butter before.'* He was very excited by making butter. This perhaps meant that he had a very clear memory of what had happened previously.

Type: process skill (hypothesising based on previous knowlege and experience)

Comment

The teacher decided to make sure they discussed previous

Wednesday 27th January

To Find Out Which Cream Would make the most Butter.

Apparatus - You need 2 identical glass Jars (with lids) Why? Whipping cream &
1 tub of 5 oz Double cream.
1 tub of 5 oz
1 wooden spoon & 1 stop watch clock.
2 plates   Kitchen Scales ✓

Hypothesis - I think that the double cream will make the most butter. Because the double cream has got more fat. and its winner than whipping the Whipping cream ✓ Method - We split the cream in half the Them to Jars and and put it in really hard shaked we opened the lid

Then we got some cream crackers to test witch one tastes the best and I think which that the whipping cream taste very nice. Results - My hypothesis was nice right gerest about I won the two cream because the double cream had more butter than the whipped cream it had 3 oz and the whipped cream had ½ oz

Double cream WON!!!!

WHIPPED CREAM   Double CREAM   Double cream   Double Butter

Whipped Cream   Very good pictures are important in science   Whipped cream

Jars   CREAM CRACKERS   Cream Crackers

experience explicitly before embarking on investigations in class. She talked with Andrew about how he had made his test fair.

Physical Processes

Lucy (Reception): *Investigating magnetic and non-magnetic materials*

Lucy sorted objects into two sets: *'these did stick to the magnet'* and *'these didn't stick to the magnet'*. She quickly pointed out that the set of objects that *'stuck'* to the magnet were all metals. She also noticed that there were metals in the *'did not stick'* set, but couldn't offer an explanation. The teacher then gave her a lock component made of two different metals. Lucy observed the magnet stuck to one part and not another. She said *'It's different metal'*.

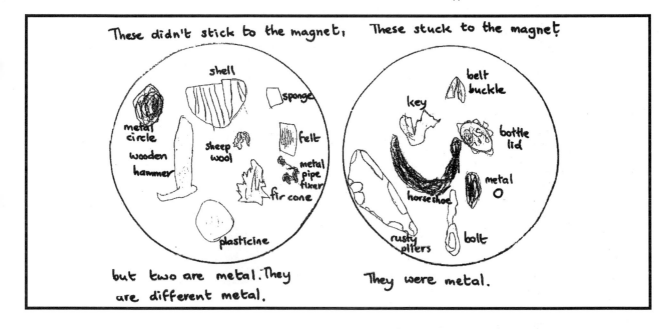

Why was this significant?

Lucy was able to offer an explanation. She realised that metals do not all behave the same when using magnets.

Why did it happen?

Lucy said she noticed the metals in the lock component were different colours and then thought *'it must be different metals'*.

Type: concept clicking (recognised that not all metals are magnetic); the example also shows **process skill** (hypothesising).

Comment

Lucy needs further opportunities to explore the effects of magnets on different metals to test out her hypothesis.

The careful choice of materials by the teacher to include the lock made of two *observably* different metals helped to challenge and develop Lucy's thinking. Lucy needs further opportunities to explore the effects of magnets on different metals to test out her hypothesis.

Melanie (Reception): *The Sun*

Melanie drew a picture of the shining Sun with an arc coming off it. The class topic was 'Earth in Space', and the teacher had shown the children her astronomy books and posters. They gasped when they saw the photos of what's out there. One of the photos showed the Sun with an arc of plasma just like Melanie's picture.

Why was this significant?

Melanie usually draws the Sun as a circle with spikes coming out of it.

Why did it happen?

Melanie said *'I'm always going to draw it like that, because that's what it really looks like.'* The teacher asked *'How do you know?'*. Melanie replied *'Because you showed us all those photographs'*.

Type: process skill (observations of what the Sun looks like): Melanie compared the pictures of the Sun with her previous ideas about its appearance.

Comment

The teacher encouraged the children to discuss and describe other features of the posters. It would be possible to develop this idea by asking children to draw or describe what they think something looks like, asking them to compare this with the object or photographs and considering the differences.

*This may be part of the process by which children begin to recognise the difference between the stylised representation of objects often used in books and what you actually observe directly or from photographs. (NB: It is vital that children **never** look directly at the Sun. This will damage their eyesight.)*

Sarah (Year 1): *Shadows in the playground*

The class had been out in the playground taking photos of shadows and chalking round them. Sarah drew a picture of her shadow in the correct position (upside down and attached to her feet) with the Sun in the right place (see over).

Why was this significant?

Previously Sarah had drawn shadows standing next to her, not attached – like two people standing next to each other.

Why did it happen?

Sarah said '*I saw my shadow in the playground.*'

Type: concept clicking (position of shadows); the example also shows **process skill** (focused observation).

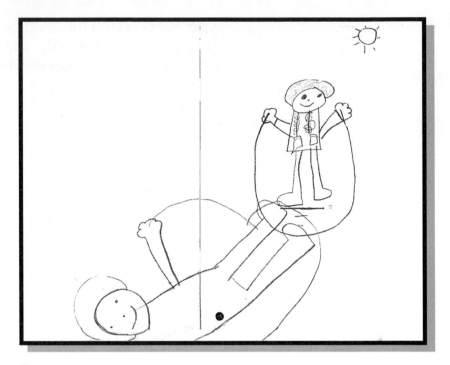

Comment

Although Sarah has noticed where shadows fall, her shadow is not coloured in black and has facial features more like a reflection. Is this deliberate? Questioning may reveal further ideas Sarah has about shadows. She could go back into the playground, observe shadows again and consider some of the following questions: *What do they look like?, What colour are they?, Can you see your features?, How do they differ from reflections?*

First-hand experience coupled with focused observation prompted by the teacher has an important role in developing ideas. Research has found that children often confuse shadows with reflections.

It is important to be cautious in interpreting children's drawings in science. Young children may have different purposes in drawing from that intended by the teacher. Sometimes they represent objects in symbolic or imaginative way or seek to indicate their knowledge about an object (e.g. that they have a nose, mouth, eyes) whereas the teacher may be expecting children to record only what can be observed directly. Further questioning can help to sort this out.

Peter (Year 1): *Exploring sounds*

The children were asked to explore a range of instruments and to identify which produced high notes and which low notes. The children recorded their findings in drawing and writing. Peter is Russian and new to English. Through his drawing, labelling and discussion he showed he had grasped the concept of low and high notes and understood the words 'high' and 'low' in English.

Why was this significant?

His work showed understanding of the concept of high and low notes. Peter was able to use the words 'high' and 'low' appropriately.

Why did it happen?

Peter seemed interested in the task. He was working in a practical group situation where children were sharing and demonstrating their understanding. The teacher gave Peter examples to illustrate these words and encouraged him to find others.

Type: concept clicking (an instrument can give out a note when played; notes can vary in pitch from high to low)

Comment

Introducing new words and concepts in a practical context through examples went well and gave Peter access to the task. It will be important to use this approach in future wherever possible, and to identify the key words to emphasise in each topic. Working in a group, Peter was able to share and develop his ideas. Giving feedback to the group on how well they worked together may encourage others to give similar support in future. Peter needs opportunities to explore other properties of sound, different ways of making sound and how the sounds/notes an instrument produces can be changed.

Introducing new ideas and scientific vocabulary in a practical context is a strategy that is important and effective not only for bilingual pupils. As a largely practical area of the curriculum, science offers exciting opportunities for the involvement of bilingual pupils and for language development.

Jo (Year 2): *Making circuits*

Jo made a circuit with a battery, bulb and a switch. She recorded her circuit.

Why was this significant?

Jo is usually unable to record investigations and her drawings are often inaccurate representations of what has happened. In this case she recorded confidently and accurately:

❛ *You get one wood then you get a battre. Then you get a light bulb then you get a paper clip then a wrye. Then the light bulb lit you wyre then off then on.* ❜

Why did it happen?

Jo said '*I know because my dad bought me a book.*'

Type: process skill (recording); the example also shows **attitude development** (increased confidence) and **concept clicking** (how to make a circuit).

Comment

Jo needs opportunities to build on her knowledge of electricity – making switches and more complex circuits. It is important to give feedback to Jo's dad about the positive effects of his involvement and find ways to support this in future, for example by encouraging Jo to take home books on classroom topics to share with her parents, inviting her to talk about experiences she has at home, and developing a dialogue with her parents, sharing her work and progress in science.

Parental interest can have a marked effect on children's progress. Two publications that provide useful suggestions about ways of involving parents in science are referred to in Chapter 6.

Alan (Year 2): *Testing which materials conduct electricity*

Alan tested a range of materials to find out if they conducted electricity, and recorded his findings. The teacher indicated that he could only do this if he was listening and completing his work as he went along.

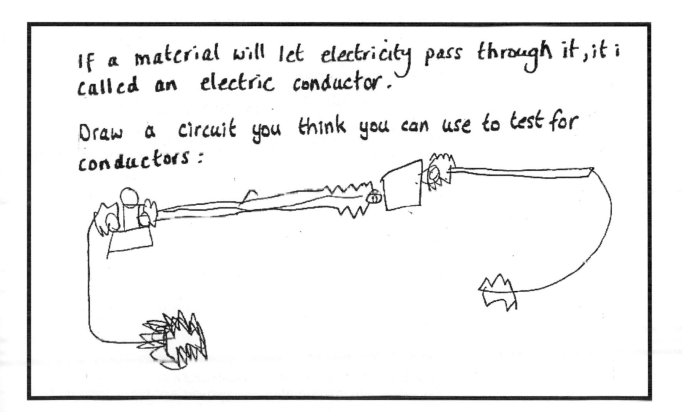

Which of these materials do you think will conduct electricity?

copper wire, yes ✓

plastic NO ✓

paper yes ✗ no

tin foil yes ✓

paper clip yes ✓

wood no ✓

leaf yes ✗ no

wool yes ✗ no

✓ good.

Why was this significant?

Alan sustained a much greater level of interest, motivation and concentration than usual. He achieved much more than is often the case.

Why did it happen?

Alan said he really wanted to test the materials.

Type: attitude development (perseverance, curiosity); the example also shows **process skill** (predicting, recording) and **concept clicking** (materials that conduct electricity).

Comment

The combination of an activity that Alan found interesting with a clear task and expectations helped to produce positive results. It is important to find contexts that motivate Alan and to set clear short-term targets. Looking at Alan's records of his predictions and findings, it would be interesting to ask him how his ideas about what conducts electricity have changed.

Exciting first-hand experiences that build on children's interests play a key role in promoting development in science.

Samir (Year 3): *Floating and sinking*

The children were given a variety of materials to test out in the water tray. The teacher provided a series of questions to help the children focus on what they had found out about floating and sinking. Samir drew up a list of conclusions from his investigations.

Floating and sinking

1. I think that cylindrical shapes float better in water.

2. Not all flat things float. Not all round things sink.

3. Not all heavy things float

4. If you drop a heavey thing on the water it would splash.

5. You can mack floating sink by bending or cuting something.

6. Shapes can chage eg sinking to floating.

7. No, pastine does not float

8. Put all objects in fairly.

Why was this significant?

The results were presented very clearly. Samir showed his ideas about floating and sinking had developed considerably.

Why did this happen?

Having the list of questions helped Samir to focus on his findings.

Type: concept clicking (factors that affect floating and sinking); the example also shows **process skill** (interpreting).

Comment

Carefully structured materials and focused questioning both played an important role in the development of Samir's ideas. This approach could be used again in future. It would be useful to compare the results of different children. Did anyone make the plasticine float?

Sandra (Year 4): *Batteries and bulbs*

Sandra followed through her ideas into a practical investigation of the effects of varying the number of batteries and bulbs in a series circuit.

Why was this significant?

She noticed relationships between the brightness of the bulbs and the number of bulbs and batteries in a circuit:

❛ *Two battarys one bulb quit brit . . . We put two bulbs and two battarys on so our light got dimer and used up more light and battary.* ❜

Why did it happen?

Sandra said that she had done some work on electricity at home, but working with her partner Susie had helped her realise what was happening.

Type: concept clicking (effects of more batteries or bulbs in a circuit)

Comment

Building on work done at home and working with her partner helped Sandra to notice patterns in her observations. In future she could compare series and parallel circuits and develop ideas of resistance in a circuit.

Daniel (Year 4): *Floating and sinking in salt water*

The children were working in a small group, trying to find out how the amount of salt dissolved in water affected the level at which a piece of wood floated. They added 5ml of salt at a time to water in a jug and measured the level at which the wood floated. To start with, they noticed that for each 5ml of salt added, the wood floated 1 cm higher. However, after 15ml the wood did not float any higher and when they added 100ml it still made no difference.

> We think that every 5ml of salt we put in the wood floats 1 cm higher. So now we're going too put 10 ml of salt in the jug and see if it goes up two cm. We found out that if we put 100 ml of salt into a jug it does not desolve and it didn't make it float any higher. We think that it makes the water more thicker.

What was significant?

Daniel offered an explanation for his findings. He suggested that the extra salt did not dissolve and so did not make the wood float any higher. He thought the salt made the water 'thicker'.

Why did it happen?

Daniel said '*I was trying to work out why the wood did not go any higher.*'

Type: **process skill** (hypothesising) and **concept clicking** (there is a limit to the amount of substance that can be dissolved in a given amount of water; the 'thicker' the liquid the higher the wood floats).

Comment

Setting Daniel exciting problems to solve and explain helped to promote developments in his thinking. He could test out his ideas by investigating the amounts of other substances that will dissolve in a given volume of water, or by exploring floating and sinking in other (thicker) liquids, such as oil, glycerine and washing-up liquid.

Chris (Year 4): *Steeper slopes*

Chris's task was to find out how much force was needed to pull a tin of sand up a slope using a spring balance. He set up the investigation for himself, choosing his own equipment and tabulating results.

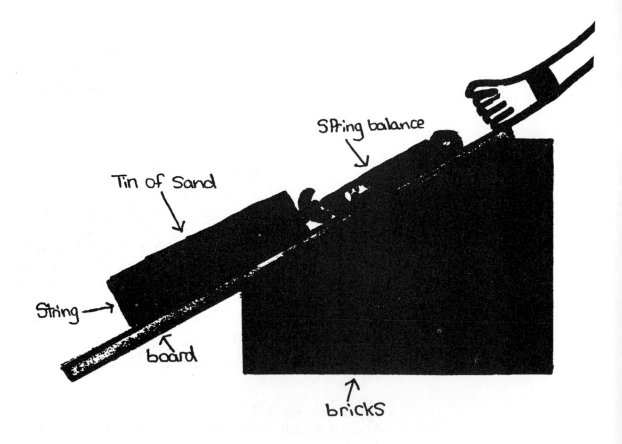

Why was this significant?

He set about the task in a very systematic way. His drawings were more precise than usual, and he tried using extra bricks on his own initiative.

Why did it happen?

He has done similar work on a flat surface. He said he used this past experience to help him.

Type: process skill (planning and recording an investigation)

Comment

The teacher planned to observe if Chris could adopt a systematic approach in a new area of study.

Undertaking investigations in a familiar context, similar to those they have tackled before, can provide valuable opportunities for children to apply new skills and develop confidence and independence.

Narges (Year 4): *Storing energy in plastic crawlers*

Narges worked with a group to explore storing energy in a plastic crawler. She made her crawler using specific equipment. The group tried out various investigations – seeing if it would go up a slope or pull a load, finding out how far it went with different numbers of turns of the elastic, etc (see over).

Why was this significant?

Narges led the group, which was unusual.

Why did it happen?

The children had been asked to take turns in leading.

Type: social skill (taking a leading role in a group)

Comment

It will be important to continue to emphasise taking turns and to congratulate Narges for taking a lead.

Setting a clear framework for allocating tasks can give children support to undertake new roles, helping to ensure that the same children are not always directing activities. It can be particularly important to ensure that girls have opportunities to take a lead in physical science tasks.

Sara (Year 5): *Cars down the ramp*

Sara investigated how far her car travelled as she changed the height of the ramp and the weight of the car (see over). The teacher asked her to explain what she had found out. Sara said '*As the ramp went higher, the car went further.*' The teacher then asked her if this was what her results showed. Sara noticed '*The numbers don't go up*' (the results do not show any clear pattern) and '*It's not really a fair test*' (she changed both the weight of the car and the height of the ramp).

Why was this significant?

She looked critically at her results rather than just ignoring them and repeating her original idea.

Why did it happen?

Sara said '*The equipment was easy and fun to use. I knew what I was looking for.*' The question the teacher asked encouraged her to focus on her findings.

Type: **attitude development** (respect for evidence and critical reflection); the example also shows **process skill** (interpreting results).

Comment

Sara needs an opportunity to repeat her investigation, making sure it is a fair test, checking and repeating measurements as she goes along. She could test out possible explanations for her results such as:

◆ The last four measurements were recorded incorrectly, leaving out the 100 (writing 49 inches instead of 149 inches) (NB familiarity with Imperial units in daily use is required by the National Curriculum).
◆ Once the ramp had gone beyond a certain height, the car no longer moved smoothly from the ramp to the floor, but bumped at the bottom of the ramp and therefore did not travel so far.
◆ The car was very variable in its performance, so for a given ramp height the car might travel a wide range of distances. This indicates a need to repeat measurements and take an average.

Size	7½	7½	7½	7½	7½	7½
height	9 inch	10 inch	14 inch	17 inch	21 inch	23 inch
weight	34g	34g	34g	50g	52g	60g
time	4 SC	3 SC	3 SC	2 SC	2 SC	2 SC
lowFat	140 inch	150 inch	139 inch	139 inch	49 inch	48 inch

Size	7½	7½
height	27 inch	28 inch
weight	67 g	85 g
time	2 SC	2 SC
howFar	41 inch	38 inch

conclusion

AS the Ramp went higher the car went Further.

When asked to report on their findings, children often repeat their predictions or base their comments on qualitative observations rather than looking at patterns in their actual measurements. As indicated in Chapter 2, this is an important area to work on with children. Discussing and exploring reasons for unexpected results can do much to further children's understanding of investigations and may lead to new findings.

Tom (Year 5): *Spirals*

The teacher had set up a group activity investigating spirals made from different materials. The children added paper clips to the end of their spirals and measured how far they stretched. Tom said *'The paper one will stretch the most because it's more bendy. The others are stiffer.'* He drew a graph to show what happened to the different spirals and interpreted his results.

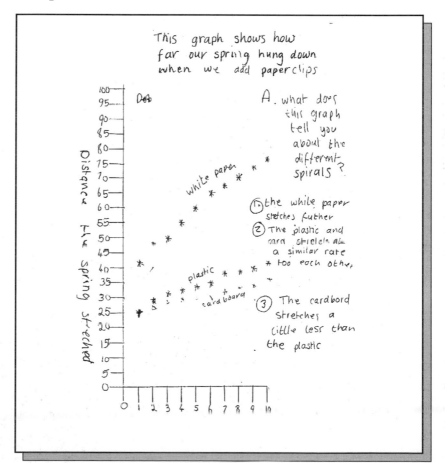

Why was this significant?

Tom was able to interpret his graph, comparing not just how far the different springs stretched but the rate at which they stretched as more paper clips were added.

Why did it happen?

The teacher asked the children to focus in particular on interpreting their results.

Type: process skill (interpreting results)

Comment

The task and method of recording were given by the teacher. They were taken from Johnsey (1992) *Primary Science Investigations* (Simon and Schuster). This enabled the children to focus on accurate measurement and the interpretation of results.

Malcolm (Year 6): *Bridging the gap*

Malcolm carried out an investigation to find out what kind of support would make his bridge the strongest. He carefully measured the load each bridge would take and recorded his findings systematically.

Why was this significant?

Malcolm took particular care in measuring and recording the load each bridge took before collapsing.

Why did it happen?

Malcolm said he talked with his partner and they decided what to do.

Type: process skill (measuring and recording)

Comment

The teacher decided to share and discuss the different methods of recording used by the class and to compare results.

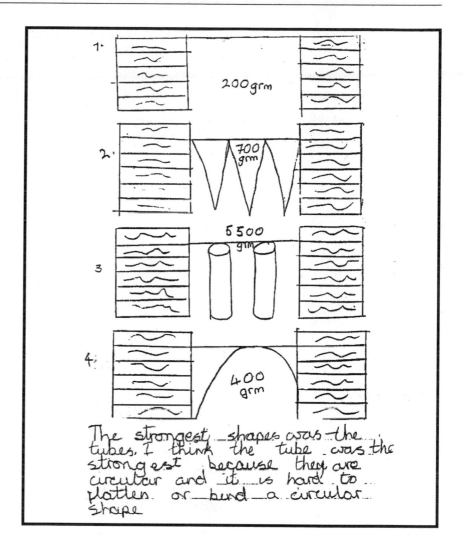

The strongest shapes was the tubes. I think the tube was the strongest because they are circular and it is hard to flatten or bend a circular shape

Establishing a classroom climate in which children collaborate effectively can do much to enhance the quality of children's investigations.

Rahima (Year 6): *Exploring lenses*

Rahima was involved in investigations into lenses. She collaborated effectively with her group and focused well on the task. She undertook the role of scribe and negotiated where to go next with the class teacher. Her recording was accurate, showing good use of scientific language. Rahima demonstrated a willingness and ability to ask her own questions. The children used reference material in the classroom to support their investigations.

Why was this significant?

Rahima had a negative self-image in science. In taking over the role of scribe and negotiator for her group, and in producing work of quality, Rahima indicated a new confidence. At times in the past Rahima has found it difficult to work well with others. In this case she collaborated very effectively with her group.

Why did it happen?

At the start, the children with whom Rahima normally worked formed a different group. At first this seemed to demoralise Rahima, but the class teacher persuaded her to work with some other children exploring the different images formed by different kinds of lenses.

Type: social skill (cooperation); the example also shows **attitude development** (confidence and independence).

Comment

It will be important to consider future groupings for

activities in the light of Rahima's success and concentration on this particular task. She could extend her work by publishing and presenting her results to the class, investigating the images produced by different shaped lenses, more than one lens and by different shaped mirrors, and considering how different types of lenses and mirrors are used in everyday life.

Different groupings can have a dramatic effect on children's achievements. It is worth experimenting with different groupings to find what works best for particular children/activities.

These classroom examples begin to show the wide range of different achievements that may be significant for different children in science. Looking across the examples, a number of common factors helped promote significant achievement:

◆ changes in class groupings;
◆ provision of exciting first-hand experiences;
◆ careful choice of tasks and materials to challenge children's thinking;
◆ teacher questions to focus discussion or recording;
◆ building on previous experience;
◆ teaching to highlight specific skills, concepts or attitudes;
◆ the involvement of parents;
◆ collaborative learning

reinforcing many of the themes discussed in Chapter 2. This indicates that significant achievement may occur because of provision and intervention carefully planned by the teacher, but that unanticipated influences such as parents, other children or experiences outside school can be equally important. Above all, the examples demonstrate the value of talking with children about their achievements. The thoughtful comments made by the teachers suggest ways in which new insights gained in this process can be used to promote further development.

This chapter has focused on individual children and what constitutes development in their own particular circumstances. The next chapter looks at development in science in more general terms, illustrating the kind of progression that might be expected in skills, attitudes and concepts through the primary years.

4 Development and Progression in Science

Introduction

Chapter 3 showed many examples of the steps forward taken by individual children in science. This chapter sets these steps in the context of the overall progress you might expect in science through the primary years. Some aspects of development in science were described at the end of Chapter 2. Here, pairs of investigations in similar areas, carried out at the beginning of Key Stage 1 and towards the end of Key Stage 2, are analysed and compared to illustrate these aspects of development.

The investigations shown are spread across the different content areas of Science in the National Curriculum and are chosen to suggest the nature of progress in a range of scientific attitudes, process skills and aspects of conceptual understanding. The investigations cover the following topics: plant growth, the effect of exercise on pulse rate and breathing, dissolving, keeping dry, shadows, and cars down the ramp. For each pair of examples, the contexts for the investigations are described, developments in attitudes, process skills and concepts indicated, and ways forward suggested. Differences between the investigations at the two Key Stages are then related to the features of development shown in Chapter 2, showing the nature of progress **FROM** Key Stage 1 **TO** Key Stage 2.

Growing Plants 1

Context

The children were growing cress in different parts of the classroom. They were asked to predict whether seeds would grow better in the dark or in the light and then record the results. Later they left some cress without water and watched what happened.

Attitude and approach

Maxine was interested to see what had happened to the cress in the dark and was very surprised that it grew. She said 'a bit of light must have sneaked in through the gaps in the cupboard'. She found it difficult to accept these unexpected results.

Process skill

Maxine **predicted** that the cress in the dark would not grow, but offered no reasons for her prediction. The investigations were set up with the help of the teacher. Maxine **observed** what happened to the cress. She **interpreted** her results, noting simple differences: 'The cress in the light grew better . . . Plants need water to grow'. Maxine **asked** 'Why do plants go yellow?' She **recorded** her predictions and results. In class discussion she said 'Plants need light and water to grow.'

Conceptual development

Maxine concluded that plants need water and light to grow well.

Ways forward

◆ promoting respect for evidence;
◆ encouraging Maxine to set up her own investigations;
◆ introducing the idea of a fair test;
◆ using non-standard and standard measures.

FROM. . .

. . .raising questions during an investigation, not in a form that can be investigated
Maxine asked why plants go yellow in the dark.

. . .offering predictions
Maxine thought the cress would not grow in the dark.

. . .planning investigations with help
The teacher discussed with the class how to set up the investigations.

. . .observing simple differences
Maxine noticed how well the cress grew in the different situations.

. . .interpreting results
Maxine noticed simple relationships – that plants without water died and plants in the light grew better.

. . .communicating using simple techniques
Maxine drew pictures and wrote comments.

. . .making simple generalisations
Maxine suggested conditions plants need to grow well – light and water.

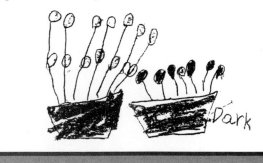

TO...

...formulating questions that can be investigated
Yogesh decided his own question for investigation.

...making predictions based on scientific knowledge
Yogesh based his predictions on previous knowledge.

...investigating independently using a systematic approach
Yogesh controlled variables, soil, type of plant, etc, considered sample size and used measurement.

...observing closely, using appropriate instruments and accuracy
Yogesh measured growth, using standard measures.

...interpreting results, making links with the original problem
Yogesh identified the best amount of water for healthy growth of his plants.

...recording systematically
Yogesh used charts and graphs.

...developing more detailed knowledge and understanding
Yogesh showed an awareness that the amount of water affects plant growth.

Growing Plants 2

Context

The children were asked to design their own investigations into what plants need to grow well. Yogesh decided to investigate the effects of different amounts of water on plant growth. He told the teacher he would compare results with Dan and Sophie because *'some plants might be different'*.

Process skills

Yogesh decided on his own **question** to investigate. He **predicted** *'If you only give them a bit of water the soil will dry up and they will die. If you give them too much they will go all yellow and floppy or maybe mouldy.'* He said he had watered his neighbour's plants when she was away and some went yellow and died because they had been watered too much. Yogesh showed an **awareness of the need for a fair test** by controlling the soil, light level, warmth and type of plant. He decided how much water to give each plant. He **observed and measured** the growth of the plants, **recording systematically** using charts and graphs. Yogesh **noticed patterns** in his results and **gave reasons** for his findings: *'1 and 2 died because they did not have enough water, 3 is growing the best because it is the right amount. 4 is not growing so well.'* He compared his results with those of the rest of his group.

Conceptual development

Yogesh offered an explanation for his results based on prior scientific knowledge.

Ways forward

◆ considering issues of sample size;
◆ further opportunities to plan and carry out his own investigations;
◆ discussing alternative explanations for findings;
◆ exploring the effects of light level and temperature on growth.

Effects of Exercise 1

Context

The class had been involved in a project on Ourselves. They had discussed external parts of the body. The teacher asked the children what they thought was inside their body and why. Vincent said *'My heart. It goes boom boom when I run in the playground. It goes fast to make me run fast.'* Towards the end of their next PE session the teacher stopped the class and asked them to lie down and listen to their breathing and heart rate. Could they feel it as Vincent had suggested? Later, on the mat, the teacher asked the children what they had noticed. Vincent said *'My heart went boom boom, then it went slow and I felt sleepy.'*

Process skill

Vincent **observed** his heart beat. He **noticed** that it went faster when he exercised and then slowed down again. He **communicated** his observations to the class.

Conceptual development

Vincent linked his increase in heart beat with exercise.

Ways forward

- planning his own investigation with help;
- using non-standard and standard measures;
- introducing the idea of a fair test;
- finding out about other internal organs;
- recording results in variety of ways, introducing tables.

FROM. . .

. . .observing
Vincent noticed changes in his heart beat.

. . .interpreting – noting simple relationships
Vincent noted that his heart went fast when he ran fast and slowed down as he rested.

. . .offering an explanation consistent with the evidence
Vincent suggested that his heart beat fast to make him run fast.

. . .communicating through talk
Vincent communicated his ideas in class discussion.

. . .making links
Vincent concluded that his heart beats faster during exercise and slowed down when at rest.

. . .awareness of external organs and some internal organs
Vincent could name external parts of the body and knew the position of his heart.

TO...

...observing using measurement
Sarah measured pulse rate using a stop watch.

...interpreting – noting patterns in data
Sarah noticed that pulse rate almost doubles during exercise and takes time to return to normal.

...explaining based on scientific knowledge and understanding
Sarah suggested the muscles would need more oxygen during the activity, so the heart would need to pump blood round the body faster and the pulse would increase.

...using more formal methods of recording
Sarah recorded her results in a table.

...applying knowledge and understanding
Sarah used her knowledge and understanding of the functioning of the heart to explain the effects of exercise and rest on pulse rate.

...explaining the functions of internal organs
Sarah showed understanding of the function of the heart.

Effects of Exercise 2

Comment

The class had been studying the body and had learnt about the function of the heart. Sarah suggested that when people are running the muscles need more oxygen and so the heart beats faster. She organised an investigation into whether exercise affects pulse rate.

Process skills

Sarah *predicted* that people running will have a faster pulse rate. She said that the blood had to be pumped round the body faster, so the heart speeds up. She *planned her own investigation*. She set up a fair test controlling the activities and the time intervals after which the pulse was taken. She considered sample size choosing two small and two tall people. Sarah *measured* pulse using a stop watch and recorded her results in a table. She *noted patterns* in her data: 'The pulse nearly doubles after exercise and after one minute it was not back to normal.' She linked her results to her original prediction and *offered an explanation* for her findings: 'I think this happened because as the heart is beating so fast straight after the exercise it hasn't yet got used to it, it will start slightly slowing down.'

Conceptual development

Sarah was able to apply her knowledge and understanding of the function of the heart to explain changes in pulse rate with exercise.

Ways forward

◆ reviewing methods critically – considering sample size;
◆ repeating measurements and taking averages;
◆ opportunities to carry out further investigations using her scientific knowledge and understanding.

Keeping Dry 1

Context

The children were making houses for three toy pigs. They were trying to work out which material would be best for the roofs. Timothy said '*It needs to keep piggy dry. Pour water on the roof and see if he gets wet.*' They decided to use a watering can to test different materials.

Attitude and approach

Timothy was eager to find out what would happen. He needed encouragement to take care in handling the watering can.

Process skills

Timothy *suggested* how to test the materials. He *predicted* the tissue paper would be soggy and the plastic would be best. Timothy *observed* that the cardboard and paper changed colour but the plastic showed no change. He *reported* '*only the plastic kept out the rain*', although both the wallpaper and the cardboard also kept out the rain. He *recorded* his test with a drawing.

Conceptual development

Timothy is developing an awareness of the properties of different materials.

Ways forward

◆ introducing the idea of a fair test, e.g. using the same amount of water and material, leaving the water for the same length of time;
◆ measuring the water in the can;
◆ considering the *full* range of results;
◆ discussing other properties of materials that influence their use at home and at school, e.g. strength, stretchiness, whether they are transparent, insulating properties, etc.

FROM. . .

. . .needing support to show care and responsibility
Timothy needed supervision in carrying out the investigation.

. . .reporting results consistent with original ideas
Timothy focused on the plastic and the tissue paper in his conclusions.

. . .predicting
Timothy thought the plastic would be best but was unable to indicate why.

. . .investigating with teacher support
Timothy suggested how the test might be carried out. He tested each material in turn with the teacher's help.

. . .observing differences
Timothy noticed what happened to the materials.

. . .interpreting, giving a partial description of the results
Timothy reported results related to his original predictions.

. . .recording using drawings
Timothy drew a picture of what he did.

TO. . .

. . .working without supervision

Lauren carried out her investigation independently.

. . .drawing conclusions, taking account of the evidence

Lauren concluded that the leather was the best and that dry fabrics take longer to soak up the water.

. . .predicting based on past experience

Lauren explicitly referred to past experience in offering her predictions.

. . .investigating independently and systematically

Lauren set up her own investigation, and was aware of the need for a fair test.

. . .observing closely

Lauren measured the time taken for the water to be absorbed.

. . .interpreting, identifying patterns in the data

Lauren noted which material took longest to soak up water and that wet materials soak up water more quickly.

. . .communicating using charts and diagrams

Lauren recorded results in a table and drew her experimental arrangement.

Keeping Dry 2

Context

The class were asked to find out which would be the best fabric for keeping you dry.

Attitude and approach

Lauren worked confidently, carefully and independently.

Process skills

Lauren *predicted* that leather would be best and linked this explicitly with her everyday experience: *'water won't get through our skin so it won't get through cow skin.'* She *planned her own investigation*, showing an awareness of the need for a fair test. She controlled the number of drops on each fabric, where the drops were placed, type of container, and *measured* the time it took for the water to be absorbed. Lauren *recorded her results systematically* in a table. She *interpreted* her results: *'We found out that leather is the best fabric for keeping things dry. We know this because it took the longest to soak up the water. The leather was more waterproof when it was dry.'*

Conceptual development

Lauren described her findings. She has not linked these explicitly to scientific knowledge and understanding of materials. Two important underlying ideas about materials are: they can be grouped according to their characteristics, and that the properties of materials influence their use.

Ways forward

◆ encouragement to review procedures critically, to consider accuracy of measurements and the need to repeat tests;

◆ opportunities for Lauren to use her knowledge and understanding in making predictions and offering explanations;

◆ further opportunities to carry out fair tests.

Dissolving 1

Context

The class were studying what happens if you mix substances in water. The teacher asked the children what different things could happen and used their ideas to draw up a table for their results. He then asked the children to carry out their own investigations in pairs.

Attitude and approach

Kim was very excited by the investigation. When the teacher asked him if he had stirred all the substances, he said '*No, I didn't*' and recognised that this was not fair.

Process skills

Kim **predicted** what would happen to some of the substances as he went along, e.g. '*sugar mixes in tea*', '*the coffee will go brown*'. He **observed** what happens as he put the substances in water. He stirred some of them and **recorded** his findings in the table. He **suggested** sugar, salt and coffee dissolved and the others didn't. The teacher asked him why he put a tick and a cross in the 'settles to the bottom' column for salt and sugar. He said '*First it went to the bottom but then I stirred it and it mixed in.*'

Conceptual development

Kim is aware that mixing substances with water can cause them to change, that some materials dissolve while others do not, and that stirring can aid the process of dissolving.

Ways forward

◆ introducing the idea of a fair test;
◆ using measurement;
◆ constructing his own tables;
◆ waiting to see what happens to the mixtures after a period of time;
◆ investigating other properties of materials.

FROM. . .

. . .reviewing methods with encouragement
With teacher prompting, Kim recognised that his test was not fair.

. . .offering a prediction
Kim predicted what would happen to some materials.

. . .observing simple changes
Kim observed what happened to substances in water.

. . .recording with help
Kim recorded his findings, using a table provided by the teacher.

. . .interpreting – noting simple differences
Kim noticed that some substances dissolved in water while others did not.

. . .describing results
Kim described his findings.

. . .grouping substances
Kim grouped substances according to whether they dissolved or not.

. . .recognising ways of changing materials
Kim recognised that mixing substances with water can cause them to change and that stirring can aid the process of dissolving.

TO...

...reviewing methods critically
Michelle suggested modifications needed to make her test fair.

...offering predictions – providing justification
Michelle predicted that icing sugar would dissolve quickest because it had the smallest grains.

...measuring differences
Michelle measured the time taken for each sugar to dissolve.

...recording using prompt questions as guidance
The teacher provided a series of questions to guide the children's reports.

...interpreting – noting patterns in results
Michelle noticed that the larger the grain size, the longer the time taken to dissolve.

...offering an explanation consistent with the evidence
Michelle suggested that the sugar crystals dissolved slowly because it took the water longer to surround it.

...recognising factors that affect the rate of change
Michelle suggested stirring and water temperature could affect dissolving rate.

Dissolving 2

Context

The teacher asked '*Which sugar would be best to use in my hot drink – castor, icing, demarara crystals or muscavado?*' The children discussed what 'best' could mean, whether sweetness or fastest dissolving, and decided to investigate dissolving. The teacher provided a set of questions to prompt the children.

Attitude and approach

Michelle *suggested improvements* to her investigation: '*We could have put the sugar in at the same time so the water did not get cold, and we could have stirred it at the same pace.*'

Process skills

Michelle *predicted* the icing sugar would dissolve quickest because it had the smallest grains. She *planned her investigation* and controlled the amount of sugar, amount of water and type of container. She *observed* the time taken for each sugar to dissolve. She *noticed* that the icing sugar dissolved fastest and the sugar crystals slowest. She *offered an explanation* for her results: '*The sugar crystals dissolved slowly because it took the water longer to surround it.*'

Conceptual development

Michelle is developing her knowledge of the different rates of dissolving of different sugars. She is aware that temperature and stirring may affect the rate of dissolving.

Ways forward

◆ investigating the effects of grain size and temperature, exploring the amount of solid that can dissolve in a given amount of water;
◆ recovering solids that have been dissolved, using evaporation;
◆ repeating and recording measurements.

Cars Down the Ramp 1

Context

The teacher had propped a shelf up against a cupboard so the children could explore what happened when you let different toys go down the slope. They tried the slope on the carpet and on the wooden floor.

Attitude and approach

At first Syreeta was reluctant to participate. She needed encouragement to have a go for herself. However, later she went back on several occasions to try out her ideas.

Process skills

Syreeta *explored* what happened when you let cars go down the ramp, working out what to do as she went along. She *observed* how the car moved, what happened at the bottom of the ramp and how far it moved on the carpet, and *described* what happened: *'My car went wiggly wobbly on the slide. It went bump, bump at the bottom. It didn't go far on the carpet.'*

Conceptual development

Her comment about the carpet suggests she is beginning to *compare* what happens in different situations – on the floor and on the carpet, and to recognise that the car goes further on some surfaces.

Ways forward

◆ promoting confidence and independence, e.g. encouraging her to work with a friend, sharing her ideas with the class;
◆ comparing different surfaces/cars/slopes;
◆ measuring the distance travelled or the height of the ramp;
◆ introducing the idea of a fair test;
◆ discussing what makes a difference to how far the car goes;
◆ encouraging explanations and questions.

FROM. . .

. . .needing support to tackle investigations
Syreeta was initially reluctant to participate.

. . .tending to look to others for ideas
At the start Syreeta relied on others to suggest what she should do.

. . .planning as you go along
Syreeta tried out different cars and surfaces in random order.

. . .observing obvious details
Syreeta noticed how the car moved, and that it went further on the floor.

. . .interpreting – making links and comparisons
Syreeta compared how far the car moved on the floor and on the carpet.

. . .describing observations
Syreeta described what happened.

. . .recognising simple relationships
Syreeta noticed the car did not go far on the carpet.

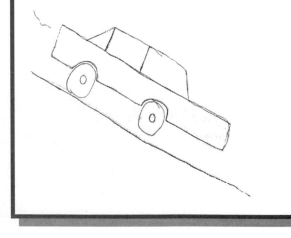

TO...

...approaching new situations with confidence
Carla worked confidently and independently.

...offering own ideas and suggestions
Carla put forward her own suggestions about what to do.

...investigating using a more systematic approach
Carla controlled variables, and measured the outcome using standard measures.

...making focused observations using measurement
Carla measured how far the car moved.

...interpreting – suggesting relationships
Carla noticed the sail shortened the car's run.

...offering explanations using scientific knowledge and understanding
Carla suggested *'The air collided with the sail to make it stop.'*

...applying scientific knowledge and understanding
Carla used her ideas about forces to explain what happened.

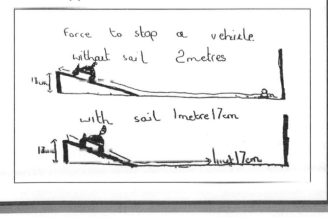

Cars Down the Ramp 2

Context

The class had been discussing what can make vehicles speed up or slow down. Carla's group decided to investigate what happens if you add a sail to a car travelling down a slope.

Attitude and approach

Carla worked with great confidence and enthusiasm. She was very much in control of the activity and listened very little to others.

Process skills

Carla *investigated* what happens if you add a sail to the car. She *controlled variables* – same car, surface, height of ramp, method of release – and *measured* the distance travelled. She *explained* her results: *'The air collided with the sail to make it stop. The weight of the car pushed against the wind, so air and the weight of the car would push against each other to make it stop.'*

Conceptual development

Carla recognised that forces can act in opposite directions and that forces can change the speed of objects. She recognised weight and 'wind' as forces.

Ways forward

◆ extending the range of measurements – varying size of sail;
◆ discussing accuracy, need to repeat observations;
◆ considering other forces that might be involved;
◆ applying her ideas about opposing forces in other contexts;
◆ developing ability to cooperate with others, e.g. producing a report jointly with others – each have to contribute.

Shadows 1

Context

The class were studying shadows. They made puppets for a shadow theatre and explored making shadows outside in the playground and indoors using a torch.

Attitude and approach

Jamie was very excited about making puppets. She worked on her own.

Process skills

Jamie *predicted* 'You will get shadows in the sun.' She *explored* making shadows with her puppet in the playground and the classroom. She *observed* what happens to the shadows indoors as the torch moved. She *noticed a pattern* in her observations: 'We moved the torch and the shadow moved.' She *communicated* her findings using drawing and writing.

Concept development

Jamie made a simple link between the movement of the torch and the movement of the shadow.

Ways forward

- observing how the shadows move, where they are in relation to the light source;
- finding out how to make shadows bigger and smaller;
- measuring the length of shadows throughout the day;
- beginning to use non-standard and standard measures;
- testing different materials – which materials make good shadows?, which materials let light through?

FROM. . .

. . .working alone
Jamie worked on her own.

. . .predicting
Jamie offered a prediction but gave no explanation for her idea.

. . .exploring
Jamie explored making shadows and using the light source.

. . .observing obvious detail
Jamie observed the movement of the shadows.

. . .interpreting – noting simple relationships
Jaimie noticed the shadow moved as the torch moved.

. . .communicating using simple techniques
Jamie recorded in drawing and writing after the investigation.

. . .identifying simple links
Jamie recognised that the position of the shadow depended on the position of the light source: *'We moved the torch and the shadow moved.'*

TO. . .

. . .cooperating with others
Ross worked well with his partner.

. . .making predictions based on patterns in observations
Ross predicted, based on previous observations of shadows: *'Shadows are long when the sun is low.'*

. . .planning investigations, working systematically
Ross took measurements systematically, moving the torch 50mm at a time.

. . .observing closely, using measurement
Ross measured the length of the shadows.

. . .interpreting – identifying relationships
Ross described the relationship between the length of the shadow and the position of the torch.

. . .communicating systematically, using more formal methods
Ross recorded his results in a table as he went along.

. . .describing relationships
Ross commented *'As the torch went up, the shadow got smaller As the torch went back, the shadow got smaller.'*

Shadows 2

Context

The class explored making shadows, using torches and objects. They then investigated how the position of the torch affected the length of a shadow.

Attitude and approach

Ross worked very well with his partner, planning together and taking it in turns to hold equipment and record results.

Process skills

Ross **predicted** *'The shadow gets shorter as the light gets higher. Shadows are very long when the sun is low.'* He **planned** the investigation carefully. He considered intervals between measurements, moving the torch up or back 50mm at a time and measuring the length of the shadow each time. He decided to **record his results** in a table. *He noticed a pattern*: *'As the torch went up, the shadow got shorter. When the torch went back, it went smaller.'* He produced a picture to show his experimental arrangement.

Conceptual development

Ross described the relationship between the length of the shadow and the position of the torch. He drew on his experiences of shadows outside the classroom.

Ways forward

◆ extending the range of measurements, repeating and checking measurements;
◆ producing and interpreting graphs;
◆ offering an explanation of the results.
Key ideas that help explain the size and position of shadows are: light usually travels in straight lines; light travels outwards from its source; shadows are formed when light is blocked by an object.

The practical business of collecting samples for these last two chapters encouraged many teachers to reflect on their own practice. Two common comments were made:

◆ Children need considerable support to raise questions and then to turn them into a form that can be investigated. The publications listed at the end of Chapter 2, such as Harlen (1985), offer useful suggestions in this area.
◆ Children rarely offer explanations without prompting. We need to encourage them to articulate and discuss their own understanding.

Hopefully, analysing development in your children's work will, in a similar way, enable you to identify areas to focus on in future.

5 Some Common Questions Answered

This chapter deals with the common questions that have emerged from teachers beginning to track significant achievement.

▶ **Does this fulfil the statutory requirements for assessment and for OFSTED?**

Yes. The statutory requirements are that assessment and record-keeping must be done in relation to the core attainment targets, but the amount of assessment and recording and the form of records is entirely up to teachers, taking account of good practice and manageability. The SCAA/DFEE Assessment Arrangements state that collections of evidence are not required, nor tick lists for each child against the criteria of the National Curriculum. You may receive guidelines from LEA advisors or inspectors asking you for some of these things, but the actual statutory requirements are as outlined here.

The significant achievement system fulfils the statutory requirements, with the tracking matrix ensuring tracking against the attainment targets of the National Curriculum.

▶ **How do you record coverage and achievement across the whole of the science curriculum?**

The Assessment Arrangements for Key Stages 1 and 2 point out the requirements, which are reflected in what follows. Your detailed planning gives you a good picture of the range of experiences that have been provided for the children in your class. If work has been appropriately differentiated, you will also have an idea of the child's capabilities. The child's ongoing classroom work and your marking comments will be another valuable indicator of particular strengths and weaknesses across the science curriculum.

Each child's Record of Achievement (if you choose to keep them, as they are not statutory), containing examples of significant achievement, will show the kind of progress a child has been making, the quality of the work, the child's views on his or her significant progress, particular conditions that support learning and ways forward. These sources of information will provide you with more than enough material to help you plan future learning experiences or report on progress. See the SCAA/DFEE Assessment Arrangements booklets for the statutory requirements for assessment, in which they point out a number of times that you are *not* required to keep detailed checklists or collections of evidence, but rather some form of assessment and record-keeping which tracks progress against broad aspects of the programmes of study only (e.g. the attainment targets).

▶ **How many times do you have to see significant achievement to write it down?**

You need to define the significance. For instance, it might be significant for a child to hold her pen properly for a short period of time and should be recorded as such, even though she may go back to holding it wrongly afterwards; it is at least a first step. The next significant achievement for that child would probably be when you notice that she is now holding the pen properly all the time. Recording significant achievement has a formative purpose – it aims to support the teacher in planning the next step for the child. This is quite different from the summative tracking of attainment in relation to the old Statements of Attainment. Then you were being asked to consider children's abilities against set criteria, which took no account of an individual child's progress towards certain goals.

▶ **I have some bright children in science who always seem to fulfil my learning intentions. Is this really significant achievement?**

This is a common comment by teachers when they first start tracking significant achievement. The first thing to do is congratulate yourself that your monitoring system (i.e. the tracking matrix) has helped you to identify this as an issue. Fulfilling your learning intentions may indeed constitute significant achievement for some children, but brighter children should be showing as much significant achievement as less able children. However, if a particular group regularly and easily do all that is expected, this suggests that children are not really being stretched and are working well within their limits. Open-ended investigations are one way of challenging such children to extend themselves, to overcome difficulties and surprise you with some new achievement. There are also all the social skills and processes involved in children organising a group when conducting an investigation or experiment in science. Teachers trialling significant achievement found that they often needed to revise their plans and go back to the science Programmes of Study to ensure that brighter children were being stretched.

▶ **I don't find it easy to spot examples of concept clicking. What can I do?**

The development of concepts takes time and very rarely happens as the result of one experience. In the early stages of developing concepts, children might just be making connections between one event and another, and only gradually will they be able to generalise over a range of situations. Becoming sensitive to these early developments takes time and practice. Reviewing research findings on children's ideas can help you to identify progress (see booklist at the end of Chapter 2). Children also need to have opportunities to demonstrate their understanding, to use and talk about their ideas. Some of the strategies listed in Chapter 2 for finding out children's ideas are useful for this. Often it is the context of investigations, where children have to apply their previous knowledge and understanding, that developments in thinking become apparent.

▶ **How can I get children to come up with their own ideas and questions? I've tried, but they often don't come up with anything.**

This is very common if children are unused to offering their ideas and questions. Here are some suggestions that may help:

◆ Sometimes children are not sure what you mean or expect, so showing a questioning approach yourself and recording all questions children ask would be a good start. Many questions come up during activities, so you could begin by listening to these.
◆ Children may need considerable encouragement and a chance to contribute ideas over a period of time. Using question boards, books or postcards, so children can contribute questions throughout the topic, are some ways of achieving this.
◆ To risk offering ideas or questions, children need to believe that they are taken seriously. So, planning work based on their ideas and questions will be important.
◆ Sometimes children do not offer ideas because they are being asked for questions or ideas too soon. Children need to have had time and experience in a new area of study before being able to formulate questions.

Above all, do not get discouraged. When I first asked my class for questions I collected about one or two in a week. However, gradually they were unstoppable.

▶ **How can I stop children keep asking me what to do in investigations? They find it hard to work on their own.**

Again, this is not unusual. It takes time and experience for children to become independent investigators. The following strategies may be useful if children are just starting to work in this way:

Make sure children are clear what investigations involve. You can do this by discussing what children need to consider at each stage: making predictions or hypotheses at the start of an investigation; talking about planning – the equipment needed, measurements to be made, ways of recording, how to make the test fair; then reviewing methods and results at the end. Doing an investigation together as a class can be helpful. Prompt sheets or a display of questions can remind children of key issues to consider.

Start with investigations that are simple and straightforward.
A number of factors can affect the difficulty of a particular

investigation. If children are new to investigations, it is particularly important to consider each of these factors in turn.

Is the context familiar to the children?
Do the children have sufficient relevant background knowledge and understanding to help them get going?

What practical skills will they need?
Will they need to be able to use a ruler or more sophisticated equipment such as a stopwatch or force meter?

What kind of variables are involved?
Take, for example, investigations into plant growth: the variables involved in investigating which soil is best or where plants grow best in the classroom are fairly straightforward. You just need to decide which soils to use or which parts of the classroom to try and how to measure growth.

Investigating how the amount of water given affects the growth of a plant is more complicated. You need to decide what amounts of water you are going to use and how often you will water. You will also need to choose a measuring instrument of suitable accuracy. Working with continuous variables like these is more difficult.

Reduce the number of decisions children have to make to begin with.
For example, you could restrict the choice of apparatus, or indicate a method of recording so that they can focus on how to set up a fair test. Then gradually increase the number and complexity of decisions.

Don't leave the children too long on their own.
Break up the session, allowing opportunities for children to feed back on progress and to share common problems and useful strategies.

Talk with the children about what they are trying to do.
Use questions to help them focus on what to consider next.

Promote a supportive climate.
This will help children to feel able to make mistakes and feel confident that their ideas matter. Consider the suggestions in Chapter 2 for creating a supportive climate.

▶ **How do you record in science? What do I do about children who are reluctant to record their work?**

Firstly, there are many ways of recording in science: drawings, diagrams, writing, tables, graphs, tapes, posters, displays, to name but a few. Children need to be introduced to a wide range of possibilities, consider what is most appropriate in a given situation and make their own choices about how they wish to communicate their findings. If children can choose how they record, they can select a form of recording with which they feel confident. Often, drawings, diagrams and charts can convey information clearly, simply and economically.

Secondly, there needs to be a real purpose in recording. When I started asking children to record in science I think it often had no greater function than to tell me often what I already knew or to prove something had been done in class. Children often focused on writing a page, or producing a long description of what they did rather than expressing their thoughts and ideas. Often the recording would be done, but not discussed or used to consider future work. I had not made it clear why children were recording, what I expected or how it would be used.

Recording can have a number of purposes and we need to spell this out. *Notes during an activity* can help children remember what they have done, organise the ideas and actions and consider emerging results. *Recording after an activity* encourages children to reflect, review findings critically or consider changes in ideas. Recording can be used to present and discuss ideas with others, to debate methods and conclusions. Introducing a range of ways of recording, clarifying its purposes and showing it is taken seriously are all strategies for encouraging children to record.

▶ **How can I support and assess bilingual pupils?**

Many of the suggestions in Chapter 2 for creating a positive climate for learning provide a vital starting point in supporting bilingual pupils. First and foremost it is important that bilingual pupils feel that their language and culture are valued in school and that they have work that is appropriately challenging. In planning and organising activities, it is helpful to consider the following:

◆ Is there scope for bilingual pupils to use their first language?

◆ In what ways does the activity build on existing knowledge and understanding?

◆ How can the activity be introduced so that it is accessible to all? Consider the use of diagrams, demonstration, models, practical resources, gestures, pictures, tapes, display.

◆ Which key words would it be useful to translate and reinforce through display, diagrams or games? Make sure you identify, use and reinforce the same words each time, so that children can follow the strands in your talking.

◆ How will bilingual pupils contribute and record? Can they do this in their first language? Would tables or diagrams be useful?

◆ Is the grouping supportive – allowing use of first language, including a supportive friend or a competent user of English?

◆ How can the activity extend the child's linguistic ability?

▶ **What do you do about a child who is not showing any significant achievement?**

This shows that you have a good monitoring system (Chapter 1 talks about a summative tracking matrix). First of all, perhaps it is just that you have not noticed what the child is doing (teachers said that, to begin with, they only noticed very obvious significant achievement, then the brighter and the less able children, and that 'middle ability' children are always the most difficult to track). It could also be that you are looking for something too spectacular. Significant achievement is anything which you think would be important to write down about a child.

Teachers pick up children's responses in a variety of ways, through questioning, class discussion, children's recording or observations of how children work. However, some (often quiet) children seem invisible. It is worth planning to watch the child more closely. Track the child through the day or a week. What does the child do? Is the child involved in discussion or activities? Who does the child work with? Where does the child position him/herself? Who does he or she talk to? Is the child, in fact, making very small steps forward? Talk with the child during activities; does the child understand the purpose of the tasks that have been set? Ask the child about his/her likes/dislikes or where he/she feels confident/unconfident. This may give you some clues about what is going on. Involve other colleagues and any support staff who work with the child. Talk with parents, if appropriate.

Sometimes this investigation will produce some kind of answer – for example, a need for support or extra challenge in a particular area, the need to rearrange class groupings or tackle problems in the playground. It might suggest areas of special interest or confidence that you can build on. One teacher found that, after half a term, there were four children for whom she had found no significant achievement. Her strategy was to take each of the children aside and look through their work with them. She found, by doing this, that they had indeed made progress. The teacher then wrote some retrospective event sheets and comments on the children's work, which gave them a tremendous boost of morale. For the teacher, it was a learning experience to see that for those children the progress had been missed but was in fact in evidence.

All children should be demonstrating significant achievement, regardless of their abilities. It is simply a matter of redefining significance for that child. Very tiny steps for one child are just as significant as big, more obvious steps for another.

▶ How do you get time to talk to the children?

It is important that the idea of significant achievement is *not* seen as something *separate* or *added on* to normal classroom practice. Discussion about learning intentions and significant achievement needs to be built into the usual times we talk to children – when we introduce tasks, talk with children about their work, handle feedback sessions, manage class sharing time, mark work, etc. Then the question becomes: How do you get time to talk to children in general? Teachers spend most of their time talking to individual children in the classroom, whether they are sitting in a group or answering questions or being brought finished work. These are the natural times for an assessment dialogue to take place; it is a matter of simply changing the emphasis of the things you say, including questions about the child's views on progress in terms of the shared learning intentions (see Chapter 1) as well as the usual management or supportive general statements.

Some of the strategies outlined in Chapter 2 for establishing a positive climate for learning science – for example, fostering children's independence, encouraging work from their ideas and questions, discussing what to do when they get stuck or how they can help each other, talking explicitly with them about how you hope to work, and so on – will all help.

▶ **Do you need to moderate significant achievement, so that we all mean the same thing by it?**

The purpose of moderation processes is to establish common definitions of each level of the attainment targets within the context of children's work, to ensure greater confidence in teachers' own assessments at the end of the Key Stages.

Moderation is only appropriate where there is a set of criteria, as in the National Curriculum level descriptions, which will be used to create levels for each child at the end of each Key Stage.

In tracking significant achievement, however, although your basic framework, for most children, will be the National Curriculum programmes of study, there can be no benchmarks defining stages of significant achievement. There is no need to embark on moderation of significant achievement because each teacher is in the best possible position to decide what constitutes significance for each child. One child's range of significant achievements may only take them a small step along the development set out in the programmes of study, whereas another child might have an equal number of significant achievements, but end up much further along the way.

Very often your criteria for significant achievement will not be found in the programmes of study anyway, but are significant because they help the child along the continuum of learning in all its aspects.

It is, however, very useful to get together as a staff and share examples of significant achievement so that you can build up a clearer picture of what achievement might look like for a particular child or in a particular subject area. (See Chapter 6.)

▶ What do you show parents?

The child's record of significant achievement provides an invaluable focus for discussion at parents' evenings. It gives a picture of the whole child, shows developments that have taken place across the curriculum, and indicates the next steps that need to be taken. It can be very useful in helping parents to appreciate what constitutes progress in each subject. Schools also need to continue to produce end-of-year reports for parents which summarise progress over the previous year.

Some schools place a marker (e.g. red felt pen mark) in the top right corner of any page of a child's workbook which has a significant achievement comment on it. This gives easy and instant access to significant work in children's books, both for parents and teachers.

▶ How would you carry out agreement trialling with the National Curriculum level descriptions?

The level descriptions are intended to be used by applying 'best fit'. The idea is that you consider the whole range of a child's achievements and decide which level for each attainment target best fits a child's achievements. This should not be an exact fit, but rather the one which best corresponds to what a child can do overall.

In order to develop a common interpretation of the levels, one strategy is for each teacher to bring one child's work for the agreed attainment target to the agreement trialling meeting, with a page of prepared notes summarising the kinds of things the child can do which are ephemeral (not written down by the child but corresponding to the criteria in the level descriptions). In pairs or fours, teachers take one child's work at a time and decide what level is most appropriate and why it cannot be the next level. Groups move around the room looking at the work until all groups have seen all children's work (about four children's work for a one-hour meeting). At the end, the groups compare their judgements, opening the debate to decide the majority opinion. Any problems which occur about decisions or interpretations of the level descriptions can be taken up with local education authority advisers or SCAA subject officers.

There are, of course, other approaches to agreement trialling, some of which can be found in SCAA 1995 publications.

▶ What would a School Portfolio look like?

The purpose of the school portfolio is to provide evidence of the school's agreed interpretations of the levels. The idea is that the work agreed at agreement trialling meetings is simply placed in a folder of some kind. This can then be shown to moderators, parents, governors, new teachers or any other interested parties.

If you decide to moderate using whole collections of work from one child, the portfolio could consist of plastic punched wallets, one for each level of the core attainment targets, so that lots of work from one child can be shown for each level. This work would obviously have to be put into the folder at the end of the year when the child is no longer using it, so a reference sheet could be placed in the wallet until then.

The portfolio could also consist of a large file, with work simply stored in the file between dividers for each attainment target and for each level.

There should be, for each collection for each level, a brief note about the level decided and why it did not fit the next level up. It should also include the date of the meeting.

▶ What about the end of Key Stage and the allocation of levels?

At the end of the Key Stage your planning records, the child's work, your marking, the record of achievement and your informal observations of their progress will give you ample evidence on which to base your judgements of a child's level. These sentiments are echoed in the SCAA/DFEE Assessment Arrangements booklets.

Getting Started

The previous chapters have discussed ways of promoting and identifying significant achievement in science and have examined examples from the classroom. The question then is: How do you get started? How can you begin to track significant achievement in your class or school? How do you create the conditions for significant achievement to occur? This chapter offers some suggestions based on the experiences of teachers who have been involved in courses on significant achievement.

Getting Started: some general principles

In planning the introduction of any change or new development, such as tracking significant achievement, the following general principles are useful:

Build on what you are doing already

Many elements in the approach to tracking significant achievement discussed in this book are not new. The approach draws on many developments in primary practice in recent years, for example:

◆ a more consistent approach to planning;
◆ the increased recognition of the need to clarify learning intentions;
◆ the involvement of the *child* in assessment – for example: through the *Primary Language Record* (CLPE 1988) or the use of self-assessment sheets in mathematics;
◆ the development of pupil profiles and Records of Achievement;
◆ the discussion of dimensions of learning, as for example in *Patterns of Learning* (CLPE 1990).

As a result, there may be many aspects of your current practice that you value and can build on. It is therefore important to begin by reviewing what you do already as a school or class, and considering how it could be extended or modified.

Start small

Trying to introduce a complete change in practice overnight is a daunting prospect, and rarely effective. Starting small gives teachers the chance to experiment with different approaches and techniques, share problems and evolve an overall system that fits their own school policies and situation. You could begin with a small pilot project on significant achievement: tracking significant achievement in your class for a few weeks, concentrating on one area of the curriculum or involving a small group of interested teachers. Some teachers have introduced the idea of significant achievement to their schools by working with interested colleagues and then gradually involving the whole staff.

Begin with areas of strength and extend outwards

In taking on any new idea, building on areas of strength gives you the best chance of success. Many teachers when starting to consider significant achievement have begun by concentrating on language development, as this is the area in which they feel most confident and have the clearest view of children's progress. They have then extended the same approach to other areas of the curriculum.

Make time for regular review

As new practices are introduced and implemented, ideas often change and develop. Further suggestions emerge or unanticipated problems occur. People can become discouraged by difficulties or lose focus once the initial enthusiasm wears off. Planning opportunities to review what has happened and share experiences can enable teachers and children to refine their approach, regenerate commitment and have a sense of their own progress with this new venture.

Getting Started: examples of practice

Over the past year teachers have shared with us the differing ways in which they have introduced the idea of significant achievement in their classes and schools and have begun to develop their practice in science. The following suggestions are based on their ideas and experiences.

Getting started with your class

In the early stages, teachers reported that they had tried to promote and identify significant achievement in their classes by:

Focusing more explicitly on learning intentions

◆ clarifying learning intentions at the planning stage;
◆ sharing learning intentions with the children in a variety of ways – through talk, writing, display and questioning;
◆ planning time to review learning with the class and individuals.

Introducing the idea of significant achievement to the class

◆ talking with the class about significant achievement;
◆ sharing examples of children's work over the last year, since they came to school or from the infants/nursery – discussing how the examples differ, e.g. introduction of fair testing, more accurate recording, use of measurement, increase in number or quality of explanations or questions;
◆ making decorated sheets and folders to record and store examples of significant achievement;
◆ setting up a display or notice board about significant achievement, linking this to learning intentions;
◆ establishing a sharing time for children to talk about things they are proud of.

Tracking significant achievement

◆ monitoring significant achievement for a month, examining the pattern for individuals and areas of the curriculum (using the grids from Chapter 1);

◆ identifying individuals or areas of the curriculum that need further attention;
◆ tracking the significant achievements of 3-4 children in detail.

Taking time to discuss children's work

◆ making notes of significant achievement on children's work *at the time*;
◆ referring back explicitly to learning intentions;
◆ indicating not just *whether* the work was good or not, but *why* and *in what ways*;
◆ drawing attention to positive examples of work, both during and after sessions.

Involving children in decision-making

◆ sharing ideas for planning at the start of a project or activity;
◆ discussing improvements in classroom resources and their organisation;
◆ explaining the need to talk with groups/individuals about their work;
◆ talking about how children can help and support each other.

Considering the whole child in context

◆ focusing on the development of skills, as well as knowledge and understanding;
◆ recognising the importance of attitudes and approach to learning;
◆ examining classroom groupings more critically;
◆ considering the involvement of parents.

Reviewing progress

◆ encouraging children to identify their own significant achievements;
◆ getting feedback from children about the effects of focusing on significant achievement – many noted a considerable increase in confidence and self-esteem;
◆ noting individuals *not* making significant achievement;
◆ sharing successes and progress with the class.

Getting started with the school

Teachers used a number of different strategies for introducing the idea of significant achievement in their schools. They:

- **introduced the idea of significant achievement** using the framework described in Chapter 1;
- **shared examples of significant achievement** from their own classrooms or the course;
- **asked teachers to bring their own examples** of significant achievement to a staff meeting, sharing ideas and difficulties, and identifying common patterns;
- **reviewed current practice** in planning, assessment and record-keeping;
- **discussed ways of building a focus on significant achievement into aspects of current practice**, e.g. planning cycle and proformas, current observation and sampling procedures or systems of record-keeping;
- **trialled the approach for half a term**, identifying groups/areas of the curriculum where significant achievement is often not observed;
- **planned INSET to focus on areas of concern**, for example mathematical or scientific investigations, extending able pupils, and assessing bilingual learners
- **exchanged examples of progress** regularly, both formally and informally;
- **discussed what should be passed on to the next teacher**, each teacher bringing a child's record of achievement to a meeting and swapping records with a colleague, deciding what would be useful.

Developing science in the classroom

In trying to promote significant achievement in science, teachers indicated that they were:

Doing more investigative work

- starting in contexts familiar to both pupils and teacher;
- trying the investigation out first, sometimes with a very small group;
- allowing time for children to explore materials first, to encourage children's own questions and hypotheses;
- providing support in investigations: discussing explicitly

what is expected, using prompt sheets or questions, and stopping periodically to review progress;
- ◆ gradually building up independence by increasing the number of decisions children have to make, reducing the support provided;
- ◆ planning time for review and evaluation.

Starting from children's ideas

- ◆ finding out ideas at the beginning of a topic or activity;
- ◆ at first planning activities for the children based on these, but gradually involving children more in decisions;
- ◆ listening more to children.

Organising resources and displays

- ◆ planning stimulating materials and displays to start the topic;
- ◆ finding more measuring equipment;
- ◆ labelling resources and materials;
- ◆ encouraging children and parents to bring in resources.

Involving parents

- ◆ displaying a planning poster with learning intentions clearly indicated;
- ◆ setting up a classroom display of children's significant achievement in science;
- ◆ sharing examples of significant achievement in science with parents, both informally and formally.

Some schools have organised parents' workshops, open days/evenings or science weeks. Some have suggested activities that children could try out with their parents at home. The Association for Science Education (ASE) has produced two publications that provide useful ideas for working with parents in science:

ASE (1991 and 1992) *School Home Investigations in Primary Science* (three books)
ASE (1992) *Primary Science: A shared experience*

Above all, by listening to children and encouraging them to offer their ideas, as time went on teachers reported seeing far more examples of significant achievement in their own classrooms.

*Only you and your immediate colleagues can decide how best to apply the principles involved in tracking significant achievement in your own class or school. It is important that you let these principles guide the style and formats you adopt for recording purposes, rather than making the recording system the first point of reference. And although the approach to assessment outlined in this book more than satisfies statutory and inspection demands, some educationists and others will always ask for paper-and-pencil statistics, in order to satisfy their own agendas. We must make sure that they do not lead us to focus on meaningless marks on paper, when our duty is to help to further children's **learning** to the best of our ability.*